B

AND
BANDAGES

— KATHY —

ALL GAVE SOME

SOME GAVE ALL

Semper fi

Dell Allen

Dell

First Printing

ISBN-13: 978-0692701553

ISBN-10: 0692701559

Easytime Publishing

Easytime Publishing

www.EasytimePublishing.com

From the Civil War to Afghanistan

2,012 Hospital Corpsmen

lost their lives

During the Vietnam conflict

639 Hospital Corpsmen were

Killed in combat

Four Corpsmen involved in the

Vietnam conflict were awarded

The Medal of Honor

PROLOGUE

May, 2016

Forty-eight years ago on a day in May, I returned to my family from the Republic of South Vietnam.

I also returned to antiwar protesters walking in the streets and on college campuses. Soldiers, Marines, Sailors, and Airmen bought the freedom for them to voice their opposition to the conflict in Viet Nam. Veterans either melted into society or displayed the slogan of the day.

AMERICA----LOVE IT OR LEAVE IT

High School buddies were still driving up and down main street, USA looking for a little "action."

There was a sense of urgency. Life had nearly passed me by. I felt I was living on borrowed time and there was no time to waste.

I returned to a Human Resources Director who had graduated from college with military draft deferments.

"What are your qualifications young man?"

"Well, I can treat diarrhea and gonorrhea, give injections, cure infections, save lives and take lives, hand out salt pills, cook ham & mothers in a can and sterilize your water with iodine so you don't get the squirts."

"Sorry. We'll be sure to call when we have another war."

I returned with a maturity that is gained by being

exposed to the dynamics of life and death. The average third world family lived day to day in huts with dirt floors. The plight of Mama-sans and baby-sans who would treasure everything we as Americans tend to complain about on a daily basis.

Destiny became my friend. I had an ambition to get on with life. Destiny also became my demon and the demon's name was guilt. There must be a reason I had survived when so many around me did not. Will the decisions I make in life, when I have more than one option, be the right path to follow?

Please tell me it doesn't really matter.

My son asked me if I kept a journal about my experiences while I was attached to the 1st Marine Division.

I had not.

I could have said diaries were for school girls, but the truth is, I never gave it a thought. I did not perceive my service along with my father's legacy may interest future generations of sons and/or daughters.

The process began rather slowly. Uncovering the past has its consequences and I did not know what they might be. That part of my life had already been reconciled and the wounds had finally healed. Was picking at the scab all that necessary?

Hesitation evolved into an endeavor.

The following events are true to the best of my memory, how I felt at the time, and my interpretation now of those experiences.

Some I served with are not as vivid as they once were and some names have been changed to protect their privacy or have faded over time.

As a Navy Hospital Corpsman attached to the Fleet

Marine Force, I could only hope I would serve them well. I will always remember the Marines who gave their last full measure of devotion.

They will remain forever young.

ACKNOWLEDGMENTS

My thanks to those who offered support and constructive criticism. Your contribution lies within these pages.

A special recognition to my son Erik who always felt he should have carried the family's military legacy into the next generation.

Above all, to my wife Val for her love, understanding and encouragement.

CHAPTER I

March 7, 1965

Now eighteen-years of age and by law I was required to go to the Post Office and register for the military draft. There was no preconceived notion how that simple task would change my life. I had decided, however, I wasn't taking Cynthia to the Junior/Senior prom. Her goal was to be invited to the prom four consecutive years. It occurred to me the prom was more important than who her date was. Screw that.

It was also decided I would need to separate myself from the modest dairy farm that had been my home for some 16 years. It consisted of 120 acres of field and pasture that nurtured a dozen Holstein milk cows and younger generations of cattle. The milk was filtered into ten gallon cans picked up each day by a local cheese and butter creamery. A mixture of roosters and hens supplied us with meat and eggs. A one acre garden produced assorted vegetables for the winter and the cucumber patch was responsible for back-to-school clothes, pencils, and notebooks.

September of 1953

Enrolling in first grade at District 206, a one room country school house, was somewhat of a milestone for a six year old. The local farming community paid Miss Pribinow for the task of providing the children a proper education. Each morning mother would send me off with a bag of school essentials and a lunch bucket filled with a glass lined Thermos of cool-aid, a couple of peanut butter and jelly sandwiches and a home-made cookie. I, along with school mates, would walk unescorted to and from school each day without a shred of fear of the unknown. The classes consisted of basic math, reading, writing and penmanship for grades one through eight. Unstructured lessons included learning how to tie shoes, field trips in the meadows and wood lots. I soaked up the new-found knowledge like a sponge.

During my third year, District 206 closed and consolidated with two schools in adjacent towns. It took some time to adjust to school in the "city." The classes were very structured and I paid the price for my rebellious behavior. My parents were invited to the school on more than one occasion for discussions of sending me to a reform institution. That got my attention along with a healthy dose of discipline on the home front. My disrespect for my parents and teachers was met with swift and certain consequences. My father would produce his pocket knife.

"Go cut yourself a willow switch."

Of course, I would take my time hoping he would reconsider. Just in case he had not, I cut a dead willow and brought it back to him. One swat and it turned into dust. That happened only once.

Eventually, my attitude improved. I also developed an interest in Margie, a petite blond who attended the same church but a different school. Not to be discouraged, I sent her love notes, valentines on February 14th and birthday cards on July 2nd. Each night in the upstairs bedroom of the farm house I listened to Dick Biandi; WLS Chicago on the transistor radio. I thought of Margie as the Beatles sang "I want to hold your hand."

She never did.

Anyway, I had grown weary of the daily tasks of milking cows, feeding chickens and hauling manure. Certainly there must be places more exotic, more exciting and adventurous. My dear mother desperately wanted me to attend college in Bemidji. The problem with that idea was I had no interest in sitting in classrooms when I didn't have a clue why I was there.

I would secretly admire my father's Army uniform with all the stripes and ribbons; reminders of yesterday and faraway lands. He was assigned to Company G, 164th Infantry, Americal Division, and served during WWII in the south pacific on the Islands of New Guinea, Guadalcanal, and Bougainville. He was wounded by a Japanese sniper on the island of Leyte in the Philippines.

One week after graduation I traded my pitch fork for a suitcase and boarded a Greyhound bus for Racine, Wisconsin. Renting a room from my mother's sister, I worked nights at J. I. Case/Clausen fashioning parts for tractors and machinery. The hourly wage covered my board and room along with a used 1956 Chevrolet 2 door hardtop.

Within a few months I was called to interview for a position with the Minnesota Department of Transportation (MNDOT), the result of taking a civil service exam during my senior year. Driving from Racine to St. Paul, Minnesota, I thought I had the "world by the ass." A government job for the farm kid. It just doesn't get much better!

"What is your selective service status?" the interviewer

asked.

"1A" I replied.

"Have you heard anything?"

"Nope, nothing at all."

"Well son, I would hate to hire you and lose you to the draft right away. Let me do some checking and I'll get back to you."

A week later I received a letter from MNDOT. "You will be working for the government but not Minnesota."

My next adventure was about to begin.

Early in December, 1965 I walked with Jan, a high school buddy, into the Ottertail County Government Building in Fergus Falls, Minnesota. The first military recruiting office we came to was the United States Navy. My father's advice was, "Don't ever go into the infantry." I wasn't going to take any chances being drafted.

"What can I do for you men?"

Wow, I guess I'm not a kid anymore.

"We would like to enlist," we said in unison.

"Great, I can sign you up today. Where would you like to take your basic training, Great Lakes, Illinois or San Diego, California?"

California sounded sunny and warm. Beaches of the Pacific Ocean beats snowdrifts any day!

"Okay, I can sign you up as a Seaman Recruit or as a specialist. The Navy has many careers."

He turned to me. "How about you?"

"Well, I have always liked science and medicine."

"Great choice. There is a huge demand for Hospital Corpsmen. When you graduate from basic training you will be assigned to Hospital Corp School at Balboa Naval Hospital in San Diego."

I couldn't believe my ears.
Now this was exciting.
Sign me up!
 When do I leave?

CHAPTER II

JANUARY 2, 1966

My high school buddy's parents drove us up to Fargo, North Dakota for the pre-induction physical and swearing into the military. The physical was just a formality. They would have taken a dog with three legs and one nut.

Raise your right hand (if you have one) and repeat after me. "I do solemnly swear----and that was it. I was now the property of Uncle Sam's canoe club. We were all given a meal and a room at the Dakota Hotel for the night. The buses pulled up at 0600 hours and loaded us for the short trip to the airport. Let the excitement begin.

We boarded a Western Airlines prop jet bound for Sioux Falls, South Dakota. My first plane ride. I need to write home about this if by chance I make it to San Diego. The plane roared down the runway and groaned as it struggled to become aloft. When it finally quit shaking, a stewardess nearly the age of my grandmother offered us a soda and a sandwich. Maybe the best I can hope for is to make it to South Dakota. In Sioux Falls we boarded an honest-to-goodness jet on our way to Denver, Phoenix and San Diego.

Drill instructors from the Naval Training Center and the Marine Corps Depot Training Center welcomed us with insults. All the Navy recruits were herded to the street curb lined with blue buses. Across the street a billboard displayed a blonde California girl in a yellow bikini with a Coppertone tan.

"Take a good look men. That's the last pussy you will see for two months," bellowed the drill instructor. "Now get your candy ass on the bus."

Holy crap, what did I do to piss him off?

The buses pulled up in front of a barracks at the Naval Training Center at 2200 hours. Linen was stacked on each bunk. Most of us had never made a bed. Lights out as we shed our clothes, threw them on the floor, and snuggled in for a long nap. It had been a long day.

At 0400 hours the sound of someone beating on a metal garbage can rudely welcomed us to reality.

"Get your sorry ass outa bed and fall in outside."

We stumbled over to the mess hall for a 15 minute breakfast and then to dispersing where we were issued clothing, belts, boots, socks and underwear along with several Navy hats stuffed into a dark green sea bag. The sun was up and we were marched to the barbershop. "Next." These guys did not go to barber school. Clippers took the hair right down to the scalp. Our new wardrobe was sent to a tailors shop for minor alterations and our names stenciled on each piece. The clothes were returned to us in a pile in the middle of the barracks. The Company Commander picked up each bag and called out the name. "Johnson, Anderson, Clark, ----good god-----B---"

"Bjerketvedt, sir."

"Okay BJ."

I was tagged with BJ the duration of my enlistment.

The following eight weeks were filled with discipline, classes, more discipline, physical fitness, more discipline and intimidation.

"Your mama don't live here."

"Yes sir."

"I mean no sir."

"Suck it up sailor. You some sorta mama's boy? Drop and give me 50."

Each of us in the company were assigned a cot and locker. Our wardrobe was folded precisely and placed into the locker in an exact order. Every locker looked the same. The cot was made to exact specifications. If a cot and/or locker failed inspection, everything was thrown onto the floor and the entire company was punished. If the same person was a slob and continued to fail inspections the consequence was a "blanket party"

Lights out for the day was preceded by a recorded version of TAPS. Every person in the company shared guard duty. There was always someone on guard duty from TAPS to REVEILLE. In the very early morning hours, a group of ten or more would quietly surround the sleeping slob. A military issued blanket covered him with four guys on each side holding the blanket tight. Two other guys would put a large bar of soap inside a sock. They would clench the open end of the sock and beat the hell out of the slob under the blanket. If the slob reported it to the company commander, the guard on duty denied knowing anything about it. The message had been delivered.

Our clothes were washed on a large cement table with vents for the water to drain. The item would be soaked down and washed with soap and a scrub brush. When the item was rinsed it would be hung on a line to dry with the fly of the pants and underwear facing the Marine Corps Recruit Training center. "Piss on the Marines!" The items were attached to the line with length of white cord that was fastened to the item in a specified manner and secured with a square knot. Shinning our boots so the toes resembled high gloss plastic would take hours.

During a particular inspection it was decided my white hat was not white enough. The inspecting officer made me partially fill a pail with soap and water and stand at attention with the heel of my right foot resting against the instep of my left foot. This maneuver was called the "five and dive." He instructed me to drop my white hat into the pail, bend over at the waist without bending my knees, grab and rub my hat by the sides and recite, "Rub-a-dub-dub. Dirty pig in a tub" over and over while the entire company watched. The sweat was running off my nose and chin while the feeling was disappearing from my legs. After 20 minutes the officer yelled "ATTENTION." As I stood to an upright position, everything turned black. I vaguely remember being grabbed and laid on the ground.

It didn't matter much. It was better than milking cows, feeding chickens and pitching shit.

At the graduation ceremony we marched as a company with our flag, which were called Colors, in front of the Naval Training Center brass. I was given 14 days leave before reporting to Balboa Naval Hospital for Hospital Corps School. My parents and siblings waited for my return. It was March 1966 and of course blizzard time in the Midwest. Flying military standby took me four days to get home. Not much going on in small town USA. Attended services at the Lutheran church with the family and hanging out with my high school buddy searching for a girl that would look good in a yellow bikini.

CHAPTER III

My high school buddy's parents drove us down to the Minneapolis airport for our flight back to California. He had orders to sonar school in Long Beach and I checked into the Hospital Corps School in San Diego. I never saw him again during the remainder of our enlistment.

Hospital Corp School was a daily dose of didactic and clinical training for my entry into the Navy Medical Corps. When I wasn't in class or on a hospital ward, I lived in the student barracks. Balboa Hospital was the headquarters of the 11th Naval District. Hence, much of the superior medical officers were stationed there. The cafeteria was first class. Even the "lower than whale shit" students enjoyed eggs to order, several different entrees, and fresh fruit, all served on china.

The commanding officer of the school paid us a visit in our barracks one afternoon. After welcoming us to the school, he had some advice.

"I don't want to hear from your parents that you are not writing to them while you are here. You might have a honey you think cares about you, but when it really matters, your mother and father will always be there. Write them at least once a week. That's an order."

And then he was gone.

I did not know I would someday realize how right he really was.

I was about to graduate from Hospital Corps School. Everything was falling nicely into place. My high school teacher told my mother I would never amount to a pile of beans. I wondered what she would say now.

I received my orders to Camp Pendleton, California. WTF---? This is a Marine Corps Base. There must be some mistake. The personnel officer told me the Marines were part of the Department of the Navy. Camp Pendleton had a Naval Hospital.

Well, I guess that's not so bad.

I reported to Camp Pendleton Naval Hospital in July of 1966. I was assigned to the maximum security psychiatric service. They can't be serious. There was no training at the Hospital Corps School for psychiatry. The clients were Naval personnel who were certifiably nuts. Remember the pre-induction physical? Some judges would give perpetrators a choice; prison time or the military. Anyway, we dosed them with Thorazine which made it easier to control their behavior. Some were given the Thorazine in liquid form so they couldn't hide the medication under their tongue. Most of them walked around like zombies until their undesirable discharge. However, some refused to take the medication and they were given a choice.

"Take your medication or we will give it to you. What's it going to be?"

With the medication drawn into a syringe, we would take the patient to the floor, restrain him, and give an intramuscular dose. Some would figure it out. We didn't take no for an answer and some would get a shot every day and then be put in seclusion.

I didn't enlist for this but it's better than the infantry.

I think.

CHAPTER IV

Chieu Hoi Kit Carson Scouts

Road to Old French Fortress with dangerous bank on left

I put in for a transfer and was moved to the orthopedic ward. There were no casualties from Vietnam. The ward was for marines who had fractures from injuries as a result of "accidents". There were also nurses in white starched uniforms. Well, now we're talking, or so I thought. The nurses were given a commission when they signed on with the Naval Medical Corps. Officers fraternizing with enlisted personnel was strongly discouraged.

A Corpsmen I worked with on a daily basis was African-American from the San Francisco Bay area. We all got along very well. Waiting for a Greyhound bus in Oceanside for a weekend in the San Fernando Valley, I spotted him across the street with a group of African- American sailors. I hollered his name and gave him a wave. When we got to work on Monday we talked about our weekend escapades. I asked him why he didn't wave back to me in Oceanside.

"Hey man, I was with my brothers. You know how it is."

No. I don't know how it is. I'm a farm kid from west central Minnesota!

About the time I was beginning to feel comfortable on the bone ward, I was invited to the Personnel Office.

"Your shore duty is nearly up so you need to come in and sign up for sea duty."

I arrived at personnel the next morning after thinking about my options during the night.

"Okay, I would like any of the Hospital ships, the 7th fleet Hawaii, or the 6th fleet Mediterranean".

Two weeks later I received my sea duty orders. FMF Camp Del Mar California. Another WTF---? I rushed into the personnel office with orders in my hand. "What the hell is this? This is not what I requested."

"Sorry, Fleet Marine Force (FMF) is short of Hospital

Corpsmen. When you are done with your training at Camp Del Mar, you are assigned to the 1st Marine Division, Chu Lai, South Vietnam."

"Why are they short of corpsmen?" I asked.

"Attrition. Some have completed their tour of duty and others---well."

"Well what?"

"They were either WIA (wounded in action) or KIA."

I may have been a dumb farm boy but I figured out what KIA meant. Corpsmen were getting wasted on a regular basis. The asshole recruiter in Fergus Falls didn't tell me why Corpsmen were in such high demand. I sure hope he is proud of himself. Just saying.

Stumbling back to my barracks in a daze I struggled to comprehend what the hell just happened. My father's words kept bouncing around in my brain. "Don't ever go in the infantry." A couple days passed before I gathered enough courage to call the folks in Minnesota. My father was a stoic man and avoided phone conversations at all cost.

"Hi mom."

"Hi honey, how are you?"

I decided to try sugar coating what I needed to say.

"I'm good. I got my orders for sea duty."

"Great. What ship are you going to be on?"

"No ship mom. I've been assigned to the 1st Marine Division."

"But you're Navy. Why did they send you to the Marines?"

"The Marines need Corpsmen and the Navy attaches medical personnel to them."

"Oh, where is the 1st Marine Division?"

"Vietnam." There. I said it.

"Mom, are you there"?
"Mom?"

Camp Del Mar

CHAPTER V

Camp Del Mar lays within the massive confines of the Camp Pendleton Marine Corp Base. Camp Pendleton stretches from Oceanside, California northward to San Clemente, California.

The Marine Corps mission at Camp Del Mar was to embark on the near impossible task of molding the tender foot Fleet Marine Force (FMF) Navy Corpsmen into what resembled Marines. We were assigned to a company. Our Commander was Captain Nelson who we called Captain Crunch behind his back. He never talked in a normal voice. Screaming, ranting and raving was his specialty. Reveille was at 0400 hours. Captain Crunch screamed at us to "fall in" formation on the street in front of the barracks. We marched to the beach.

"I DON'T KNOW BUT I'VE BEEN TOLD. YOUR GIRLFRIEND'S KISSES ARE MIGHTY COLD. Sound off. ONE TWO. Sound off. THREE FOUR. Bring it on back. ONE TWO THREE FOUR, ONE TWO----THREE FOUR. Your left, your left, your left, right, left."

Once on the sand we proceeded on a two mile run. Returning to the barracks Captain Crunch screamed,

"Get your stinkin asses in the shower and fall in for inspection. You got 10 minutes." Barnholt from Arkansas looked at me.

"Jeezz, I don't think he likes us."

No shit Sherlock.

After breakfast we spent the rest of the day watching films of sanitation, hygiene, disease, and battlefield trauma. We were taught how to treat every imaginable injury from the superficial flesh wounds, amputations and horrific mutilation. The Corpsmen were responsible for the placement of piss tube and shitters on every combat base. Every person required an immunization record that recorded the shots they had received to prevent typhoid, yellow fever, hepatitis and a host of exotic diseases. The immunization for hepatitis was gamma globulin 10 milliliters. It was divided into two 5 milliliter syringes, one for each buttocks. It was the consistency of Karo syrup and it produced a serious pucker factor when it was injected. Sitting down felt like sitting on a golf ball in each back pocket. Receiving immunizations was not a pleasant experience. Each person's immunization record was part of their medical record. The medical record was secured by the medical personnel. In the event a Marine was a smart ass or insubordinate, his shot record would mysteriously disappear. They were then subjected to another series of shots. The syringes would be filled with a normal saline or sterile water solution (depending how much pain was dished out) so they wouldn't be overdosed with the vaccines. We would put a larger needle on the syringe and BINGO, attitude cured!

We would get a morning and afternoon 15 minute break from classes plus an hour for lunch. The "smoking lamp" was lit during these breaks. Cigarette butts were disposed of in a metal container. If no container was available, the cigarette was field stripped and the remains either went into a pocket or a cuff.

The last two weeks at Camp Del Mar was field combat training. The company was transported by deuce and a half trucks to a mock combat base. We set up tents and made provisions for water and food supplies. The water was contained in a Lister Bag and sanitized with iodine tablets called Halzone. It was part of the science of Preventative Medicine as it killed any bacteria consumed with the water. We were introduced to "gourmet" food in cans called C-rations.

We were sent out on patrols during the day searching for the enemy even though there were none. Ambushes were at night. Squads of Corpsmen would leave the base and set up for the night in pre-determined sites. One of the sites was on the ridge of a rather steep hill. Twenty to thirty foxholes were dug lining the ridge. These pits were a favorite hideout for scorpions. We were issued rifles with clips of blank ammunition. Under no circumstance were we to discharge our rifle at anyone at close range. We were to treat the weapon as if it was loaded with live rounds. It was inevitable some Corpsman would call the rifle a gun. Captain Crunch would make an example of him. They were ordered to stand with the rifle in one hand, their crotch in the other hand and yell, "This is my rifle, this is my gun, one is for fighting, one is for fun."

"I can't hear you!"

"THIS IS MY RIFLE, THIS IS MY GUN. ONE IS FOR FIGHTING, ONE IS FOR FUN."

The Corpsmen were called to treat fake wounds called Mulages that were applied to student victims. This became a part of practicing triage. Marine and Navy commanders would observe how each of us responded to mass casualties. Mulages of head wounds, chest wounds, and abdominal wounds with intestines hanging out like shinning snakes, amputations, chemical and napalm burns. The triage practice was performed under various circumstances. Each scenario was practiced during the day and the dead of night. Booby trap wounds, bullet wounds, shrapnel from high explosives, and burn injuries challenged the skill of the Hospital Corpsman.

"Corpsman up." Yelled a fake casualty during a fake fire fight.

It was my turn to shine. I leaped to my feet and ran to the victim.

"What the fuck are you doing?" screamed the Captain.

I turned and looked back at Crunch.

"You're dead soldier. Get your ass to the end of the line and think it over. Next".

Waiting for my next screw-up, I had serious doubts about my decision to volunteer for the Medical Corp.

Captain Crunch was again in my face.

"You're up next. We have mass casualties now, so show me if your mama gave you any brains. GO."

Crawling seemed like the thing to do at that moment. The first casualty I encountered had sustained a massive head wound. I opened my medical bag and removed a large battle dressing. As I struggled to wrap it around his head, Crunch stood over me.

"STOP!"

"Did you do an assessment?"

Damn, it's sure hard to please this son-of-a-bitch, I thought.

"Yes sir, he's got a head wound, sir."

"Well, that's pretty fucking obvious isn't it? Is he breathing? Do his pupils react to light? Did you say anything to him? Did he answer?"

"No sir, I mean I don't know, sir."

Sitting in the dirt and California sun, I'm sweating like a whore in church.

Crunch is now on his knees screaming into my ear. His face is red and veins bulging in his neck.

"Maybe your mama didn't give you brains because she didn't have any brains to give you. While you were trying to save a dead man's life, two other Marines died who didn't need to. ALL BECAUSE YOU GOT SHIT FOR BRAINS!"

At the back of the line again I felt totally pathetic. None of the Corpsmen looked at me as they were getting their ass chewed as well. Talk about a positive learning environment.

Laying in my tent that night I thought about my father's service in the military. I was the oldest in the family and I felt I had to carry on the tradition. At least I needed to try. There were military deferments granted for sons if the draft board was convinced he was needed on the farm. Those families who had the financial means to send their precious high school graduate off to college instead of Viet Nam were granted a deferment. Basically, it was a poor man's war.

If I would have knocked up my girlfriend, there was a deferment for that.

What was I thinking?

I guess I wasn't because I got shit for brains.

CHAPTER VI

Graduation ceremony from Fleet Marine Force training was preceded by one last surprise by the Captain. We marched loaded with full gear to the base of "cardiac hill"; a ¾ mile 6 degree slope. Already tired, I leaned into the hill. I had the sense the Marine Captain wanted to make a point. Eventually, we all made it to the top, albeit some crawled the last few yards! Returning from the final intimidation, we cleaned the barracks until we were confident it would pass Captain Crunch's inspection. We packed our sea bags, took a shower, and donned our uniform. We wore Marine Corps Khakis' and a hat called a Barracks Cover that was issued when we received orders to the FMF. We were not allowed to wear the Marine Corps dress blues because, after all, we were not real Marines.

We fell in formation on the street in front of the barracks. I don't remember any of us sharing what division we were assigned. Probably because we had no combat experience. We all knew it was the "Nam." We had a two week leave until Uncle Sam's Travel Agency sent us to Southeast Asia.

We stood in parade rest formation for nearly 30 minutes before Captain Crunch made his appearance. What the hell was his problem? We were more than ready to board the "bird" for home, wherever that was. Let him scream and bellow. It don't matter much now. In a few minutes we won't be missing that asshole.

"Company, attention. The company is ready for inspection, sir." The senior Corpsman saluted.

Captain Crunch saluted and walked with the Corpsman down each row of the formation. They stopped in front of each Corpsman who saluted the Captain. The Captain returned the salute and shook each one's hand.

"Good luck, make the Marines proud of you." He said in a normal tone of voice. Standing front and center of the formation, he saluted the entire company, performed a brisk left face and marched away.

"Company, fall out."

Nobody threw their hat in the air. There were handshakes, slaps on the backs, and light hearted chatter. Barnholt turned to me.

"What the hell happened to Crunch? Do you spose he found Jesus or something?"

Months later I would silently thank the Captain for pushing us in the only way he knew.

Boarding a Grey Hound bus in Oceanside, I headed for the San Diego airport. I really wanted to see my girlfriend in the San Fernando Valley but I remembered the advice of the Balboa Hospital Corps School Captain. I hadn't been home in eight months. My parents met me at the Minneapolis/St. Paul Airport which was quite an accomplishment for folks from rural Minnesota. After being reunited with my siblings, other nearby relatives along with the church congregation and pastor, my mother decided we should travel to Wisconsin to see the extended family. It occurred to me during the visit that this was more than likely a thinly disguised way of saying goodbye forever.

Walter Cronkite and Huntley/Brinkley looked at me from the television each evening. Part of their newscast consisted of the number of American casualties from previous days. A sense of doom crept into my very fiber. I didn't feel so invincible. How was I to spend a year in this apocalypse and expect to survive? Maybe my mother had a premonition.

On the way home from Wisconsin, I was pulled over by a Wisconsin state trooper.

"Son, I stopped you for exceeding the State of Wisconsin night time speed limit."

Wisconsin Troopers wear a military style "smokie" hat.

"Sir, it's not dark, Sir."

"Official sunset was 20 minutes ago. Let me see your license and title."

Returning to my vehicle, he handed me a citation. "You are summoned to appear in court in Tomah, Wisconsin on May 12th. If you do not appear, a warrant will be issued for your arrest. Do you understand? Any questions?"

"Sir, I slow down when it gets dark, sir.

"Tell it to the judge."

"Sir, I can't make that court date cause I'll be in Vietnam, sir"

"Let me see your orders."

Returning my orders, he demanded I follow him to the Law Enforcement Office in the nearest County Seat.

"Follow me and don't try anything."

Wow, he's taking this minor infraction rather seriously, I thought.

He questioned me about why the title to the car was in my father's name and insisted we pay a fine which would have taken all the cash we had. I told him we couldn't pay the fine as we would not make it home on pocket change. However, I would sit in jail over night while they put my mother in a nice motel and provide her a dinner and breakfast. The next morning we could get his cash when the bank opened.

After discussing it with the staff on duty, he sent us on our way with a warning.

"If we don't receive the fine within thirty days the warrant will be enforced. I'm serious."

"Yes Sir!" You can stick this citation where the sun don't shine, I thought. Go right ahead and issue a warrant for my arrest while I'm in Vietnam. I will be more than happy to sit in your courtroom---if I'm still alive.

CHAPTER VII

Four days before my flight date to Southeast Asia, my parents delivered me to the Minneapolis/St. Paul airport. I had resigned myself to never seeing them again. My mother had tears in her eyes and my father gave me the first hug I could remember.

Flying military stand-by into Los Angeles, California I called my good buddy's parents in the San Fernando Valley. Their son Michael, who was also a Corpsman, was stationed with me at Camp Pendleton Naval Hospital. Ted & Millie treated me like one of their sons. I would spend liberty with Michael and his family every weekend we were not on duty. Michael and his girlfriend had introduced me to her friend Cecelia. Cecelia was a stereotypical California girl, tall, blonde, tan and beautiful. She, and her young son Jimmy, lived with her mother and three younger sisters. We had dated for about eight months. Pool parties, cruising Van Nuys Boulevard, the beach at Malibu and Ventura Highway were weekend adventures.

Michael drove up from Camp Pendleton and we all spent the weekend together. Michael went back to the base on Sunday night. Ted, Millie, and Cecelia took me to Norton Air Force Base in San Bernardino the next morning. Ted shook my hand, slapped me on the back and wished me luck. Millie and Cecelia were crying. As Millie wiped tears from her eyes, Cecelia held me tight.

"Send me your address so I can write you. I will write you every day until the day you come home to me."

"Time to board gentlemen,"

Tearing myself away I told them I loved them, would miss them, and boarded the Continental Airlines. Next stop was Hawaii for refueling, then Kadena Air Base in Okinawa for equipment and supplies being delivered to Da Nang, Vietnam.

We were assigned a barracks for our overnight stay. Acting like a tourist, I decided to leave the barracks for a sight-seeing tour. I noticed the giant B-52 bombers when we landed. Walking up to the fence, I fished the Kodak out of my pocket intent on adding these monsters to my portfolio. A jeep slid to a stop behind me and military police jumped out. One MP pushed me against the fence and the other MP removed the film from my camera. "This is a restricted area. Now get your ass outa here and don't come back."

Home Sweet Home

CHAPTER VIII

The Department of Defense contracted with private airlines to transport troops to and from Vietnam. Early in the morning Continental Airlines embarked from Okinawa, Japan to Da Nang, South Vietnam. The 1st Marine Division had moved north from Chu Lai to Da Nang. I joined nearly 200 green troops bound for their destiny. Nearly two hours later the flight landed and we walked down a portable ladder onto the tarmac.

OMG, I thought California was hot. The heat hit me like opening the door of a furnace. The aroma was a putrid mixture of jet fuel and human waste. We were herded to a building on the edge of the air base where we were assigned to random combat units based upon need. As I waited for my assignment, I watched troops walking onto the plane we had just left. They were going home after their tour of duty. Luggage and what looked like caskets were being loaded into the cargo bay.

"Hospital Corpsman Berkavich."

I was accustomed to the butcher job of my name. Walking up to a table, I showed my orders, dog tags and signed a couple of forms without reading them.

"You are assigned to 1st battalion, 7th regiment, 1st Marine Division."

Following the sound of someone hollering 1-7, 1-7, I threw my sea bag up into the truck and joined a half dozen or so troops. After the driver finished a head count and roster, he eased the Six-By out onto the bustling dirt road of Da Nang. Children ran beside the truck begging for anything we would give them.

"Hey G.I. You want boom boom? I get you numba one boom boom."

The truck headed west past Hill 327 PX which was the equivalent of a military Walmart. It held a postal service, a USO club, American Red Cross along with nearly anything a twenty year old kid from Minnesota would ever want. Turning south, guards waved us through the last checkpoint into the countryside. We passed small hamlets, water buffalo, chickens, dogs, and women walking with baskets full of whatever on each end of a bamboo pole they balanced on their shoulder. There was the smell of smoke from the dried bamboo mama-san was burning to heat their food. The heat was suffocating and a slight breeze brought the odor of what must have been a septic system nearby. In all reality, the entire countryside was a giant cesspool. The dust from the truck tires floated around us for the entire 12 miles. By the time we got to Hill 55, we were covered with dirt. The number of the hill indicted its height in meters above sea level.

The truck stopped on the crest of the 1st Battalion base. The road was flanked on both sides by large dark green tents that had makeshift floors and half walls of plywood lining the interior. The north and south road entrances were heavily guarded with sandbag bunkers and sharp razor wire.

"Last one out toss down the sea bags," shouted the sergeant.

Jumping down from the truck I was met with a huge explosion. I dove into the dust inside the back tires. Already I had miraculously escaped death.

"What the hell are you doing under there Doc? That was our 105 artillery on a fire mission. The Battalion Aid Station is right over there. You better report in, change your underwear, and while you're at it get treated for shell shock."

Everyone laughed and I blushed under the layer of dust.

The Navy Medical Doctor was an officer who was the Battalion Surgeon. I found out later that he was a surgeon in title only. I checked in with him and the Chief Hospital Corpsman.

The Chief and I walked to the supply tent. I asked him why everyone was calling me "Doc".

"The Marines call their Hospital Corpsman "Doc" because you are in charge of their health. You need to make sure they don't get dehydrated. Encourage them to drink plenty of treated water along with salt pills. You are also a walking Pharmacy. When they get diarrhea you have a supply of Lomotil which we affectionately call Upjohn shit concrete. You will be issued morphine, atropine, epinephrine, antibiotics, malaria and iodine tablets. Your medical bag will have a supply of battle dressings, plasma and IV tubing, a surgical and burn kit."

"So, what's this gizmo?" I asked holding up what looked like a small cell phone.

"Oh, that's a strobe light. If you need to call in a Medevac at night, you hold the strobe high and hit the on switch so the pilot can see you."

"Okay, let's see if I got this right. Only the pilot can see the strobe?"

"Well no, anybody can see it."

I was a FNG (fucking new guy) but that sounded like suicide.

We spent a couple hours at the supply tent where I was also issued a helmet, armored vest, canteens, insect repellant, and a cartridge belt with a .45 caliber pistol and ammunition. The Chief showed me where I would sleep for the night. After tossing my new wardrobe on the cot, he invited me to spend the rest of the day at the Battalion Aid Station.

"Bring your helmet, vest, and weapon with you. You never know when you'll need them.

Spending the afternoon meeting and watching the Battalion Corpsmen, it was finally time for the evening meal. As we walked to the mess tent, one of the Corpsman asked if I had forgotten my mess kit. They each had a metal container that opened and served as the dinner place setting.

"I didn't get one. Where--?"

The Chief tossed me a can of C-ration and a P-38 can opener.

"Have a nice supper."

As they began laughing, I realized I had been set up.

Picking up a mess kit at the supply tent, I joined them for supper. I watched Marines finish their meal and dunk their kit into a tank of water that was heated to a light boil by an immersed kerosene burner. The Chief informed me the "dish washer" was monitored by the medical corps so it was hot enough to kill any bacteria.

Moving my new possessions off my cot, I laid down and tried to get comfortable. Where the hell is the pillow? It was hot and humid so I rolled up the blanket and put it under my head. I was dead tired. I closed my eyes and thought of Cecelia, my father, mother, and siblings.

The Corpsmen - Serving with the best.

CHAPTER IX

I dragged myself to the Battalion Aid Station at first light.

"Mornin Doc, how was your night at the Holiday Inn?"

I had to admit I was awake the entire night. Every sound appeared to be life threatening. Bright magnesium flares suspended on small parachutes were shot into the sky at random, lighting up the base and surrounding area. The 105's fired harassment artillery rounds toward "hot spots" at least once an hour.

The Aid Station was officially open for sick call every morning. Marines would show up in sandals to have their foot rot evaluated. A couple of Corpsmen were taking turns administering IM Penicillin for the "clap" (gonorrhea), syphilis, and any number of carnal diseases. One would give the shot while the other was drawing up the next dose. In an attempt to slow down the venereal disease epidemic, the Corpsmen would mention an antibiotic resistant strain. Once infected, the person would spend the rest of their life in the Philippines. The strain didn't exist but the Marines didn't know it. The Chief briefed me on the Aid Station protocol. Half the Corpsmen would go to breakfast while the other half attended to the various maladies. Within an hour, they would reverse roles.

"Bring your mess kit up here and we'll go grab some breakfast."

On the way to breakfast I surveyed the artillery battery

responsible for my sleepless night. A greeting had been painted on each barrel.

"HALLMARK – CARING ENOUGH TO SEND THE VERY BEST."

Returning to the Aid Station, a jeep was waiting to take me out to Alpha Company. Heading south, we left the base, crossed a bridge with guard shacks on each end, and headed into the flat countryside. As we passed a squad of Marines, the driver told me they were the mine sweeping team.

"Nobody uses the road until the engineers check for mines every morning with their detectors. The rest of the Marines are a security detail along with a Corpsman."

The terrain was flat low land sprinkled with small hamlets, large rice paddies and occasional cemeteries. Each burial site was a mound of soil with or without a marker. The ground was too wet to bury the corpses in a hole. The primary threats were a combination of snipers, booby traps and mines. The booby traps in more recent conflicts are called improvised explosive devises, (IEDs). They were fashioned from unexploded ordinance or empty C-ration cans. One of the antipersonnel mines was given the moniker "Bouncing Betty." It was buried in a shallow hole on a trail. A person stepping on the pressure plate activated the devise. When the person stepped off the plate, the mine would bounce out of the hole and explode. The result was not pretty.

At the one mile mark and a T in the road, he turned the jeep into Alpha Company. I was directed to the Corpsmen's quarters which was another large dark green tent without plywood walls. Two Corpsmen turned and just stared at me. They finally introduced themselves and showed me my cot. Home Sweet Home!

"Sorry about the welcome. You look remarkably like the Doc that was taken home last week. What's your name?"

"Just call me BJ," I told them.

What did they mean by the Corpsman was taken home? I decided not to ask.

"Well BJ, the company is assigned seven Corpsmen. There are five of us and you're number six. Every patrol and ambush includes a Corpsman. We average two to three patrols a day and two ambushes at night. We were out last night so we have the day off. You'll take my spot tonight. You won't be bored. Meanwhile, I'll show you around our little piece of paradise."

I was introduced to countless Marines during the day including the Company Commander, Captain Sampson. Captain Sampson had a sure fire way of ending the war.

"Round up all the good Vietnamese and put them on ships in the Gulf of Tonkin. Obliterate everyone and everything from the Delta to the DMZ. Then, sink the ships."

My tour guide gave me my assignment.

"Report here at the Command Center at 2100 hours. You'll hook up with Sergeant Green and his squad."

Following the evening "buffet" I laid in my cot trying to get some rest. Fat chance. Along with sweating profusely, my anxiety level was at an all-time high. The resident Corpsmen told me to tape my dog tags so they wouldn't make any noise. They did an inventory of my medical bag, removing redundant items and adding necessities.

"Close your eyes and remove the item we tell you. Practice until you know exactly where everything is. You can't see in the middle of the night and the grunts are all depending on you. All the Corpsmen teach basic first aid and CPR to the Marines. It may save your life someday."

In full combat gear, I joined the ambush at the Command Center. I felt like vomiting. A Lance Corporal whispered. "Follow me Doc. Make sure you can see me."

As we gathered at the perimeter wire under total darkness, I was an arm length away from him. This was not quite my idea of adventure. Once we cleared the wire, the squad turned north and very slowly moved along the west side of the road ditch. The squad would stop randomly for several minutes before proceeding. I heard a dull "pharump" in the distance and seconds later a loud pop high over us. Looking up the flare nearly blinded me. A quick glance confirmed I was the only one standing.

"Doc, get the hell down," whispered the Lance Corporal.

As a stationary target, I was a liability instead of an asset to the squad. I was quite certain this was not part of my training as I felt totally unprepared. On the job training should not be part of a life or death environment. Maybe they will send me home for a refresher course.

The ambush was set up between a small hamlet and a river. The Viet Cong (Charlie) used the river at night and had been visiting the village women. We settled into a bamboo hedgerow and all but three of us fell asleep. One Marine was on visual watch. Another Marine had the radio handset next to his ear. And I was shitting my pants.

The sun was peeking over the eastern horizon. We had left the ambush site under cover of darkness and were now less than a klick (kilometer) away from the main gate of Alpha Company. I was more than dead tired. I hadn't slept for two nights. I knew I couldn't go on like this. At breakfast, Sergeant Green sat down next to me.

"Doc, you look like hell. Get some sleep and we'll talk

this afternoon."

The morning was rather cool relatively speaking. As I laid on my cot, I dreaded my upcoming ass chewing. I fell asleep. When I woke up I had missed the noon meal and my stomach was complaining. Finding a C-ration can of ham and lima beans I cut it open with my P-38 also called a "John Wayne". I was getting used to the wrist action it took to operate this little engineering marvel. I dumped the contents in my mess kit, lit the blue heat tab and set the pan over it. A light breeze blew the fumes from the heat tab into my eyes. It felt as if I had a bar of soap in each eye. I stumbled blindly around trying to wipe away the sting and tears. When I was finally able to enjoy my lunch, I spooned a healthy load of ham and lima beans into my mouth. The ham was actually rancid pork fat. Aaaacht, I spit it back into the mess kit. Later, I found out the grunts called it ham and motherfuckers. Life is full of lessons!

I found Sergeant Green in the NCO tent. "You look better, Doc. Have a seat. Now I know you didn't sleep during the ambush so I'm sure you saw what the guys did when it was their shift to be on watch. The Corpsmen don't need to share the watch but most of them do. We share the watch as a unit, and when all hell breaks loose, we fight as a unit. You're not exempt. Now in a couple of days, you will be going out on patrol. Sergeant Lambert and I are on our second tour. You got any questions, ask us. Listen, we are in booby trap and sniper heaven. Their snipers are rewarded for high value kills. High value kills are the leader, the radioman, and the Corpsman."

"Wait a minute. The Geneva Convention prohibits the killing of Medics and Corpsmen. I have a Geneva Convention card to prove it."

"Really Doc? Do you actually think the gooks care about that bullshit? Listen, I want you to look like the guy in front and behind you so I am authorizing an M-16 for you."

"What about my medical bag," I asked.

"That's your problem just like the radio is the radioman's problem. We don't issue everyone a bag or a radio. Now, the snipers are not morons. They will pick out someone at random in the patrol and when they hit the mark, they keep the crosshairs on that person. The next person into the crosshairs is usually the Corpsman. Don't do that Doc, you hear me well. Wait until we eliminate the threat. You are no good to yourself or us if you're dead. You learn more from the things that go wrong than from the things that go right. Sometimes it is being in the wrong place at the wrong time. There is not a bullet with your name on it but there are a lot of bullets with "to whomever it may concern" on them. This isn't a spectator sport so keep your head down. Learn from other's mistakes. If you don't, you're a fool and most likely dead."

Terrific, I had 363 days, or less, before going home.

Part of the Addams Family

CHAPTER X

I wrote my parents and Cecelia a letter and crawled into my cot. Thinking about Sergeant Green's advice, I wondered how I would measure up. My sleep was interrupted by a loud explosion. Sitting up and looking around, I realized the other Corpsmen were still asleep. This went on for two hours until, finally, the night was once again quiet. I awoke to the sound of fellow Corpsmen having a casual conversation. The sun was up so I sat on the edge of the cot and put on my pants and boots.

"Sleeping in this morning, Doc?"

"I guess so. What time is it?"

"0800 hours. You better hustle over to the mess tent before they close."

"Roger that. Say, what the hell was all that racket last

night?"

"Oh, that was Frag Phillips. When he's on perimeter watch, he likes to throw   fragmentation grenades every half hour or so. Captain Sampson talked to him about it but his only reply was, "I thought I heard something." You can't argue with that. Maybe he did."

"Has anybody ever found a body in the morning?"

"Nope."

"You'll get used to knowing what is incoming and outgoing. They sound different."

I settled into the rotating routine of patrols and ambushes. I kept my ears and eyes open. My first GSW (gunshot wound) casualty was a black Marine named Montgomery. The patrol had stopped for a breather at its last checkpoint. It was an abandoned hamlet and the huts had been burned to the ground. The sound of "I'm hit" coincided with the crack of a carbine.

"SNIPER!" yelled the squad leader.

Everyone scrambled into defensive positions including Montgomery. I crawled over to him as he pulled up his trouser leg. His left calf had a groove in it and blood was running down into his boot. I opened my medical bag and without looking pulled out a small battle dressing. I can handle this. I applied pressure against his leg with the dressing to stem the bleeding so I could make an assessment. Only a flesh wound. I tied the dressing and secured it to his leg with an ace bandage. No more shots entered our area.

"Chicken shit VC musta di di mau."

Once inside the Alpha base perimeter, I assessed Montgomery's flesh wound. It had stopped bleeding and I could see the layer of fat tissue between the skin and muscle. I sent him up to the Battalion Aid Station for debridement and sutures. He would get some down time. Medical decisions made by the Corpsmen outranked Captains, Majors, Colonels and Generals. Infection could put him out for up to a month or longer. Adequately treated, he would be available in a day or two. Our Company Commander had the utmost respect for the Corpsmen.

I had begun to experience a problem which was becoming increasingly uncomfortable. My groin was as red as Rudolph's nose and on the verge of weeping. I had a serious case of chaff and it was increasingly difficult to keep up with the patrol. When I mentioned it to the other Corpsmen, they just smiled.

"We wondered how long it would take. The cure is simple. Get rid of your underwear."

The problem was caused by nearly always being wet. If I wasn't sweating I was in the rice paddies or streams or rain.

A week later, as my crotch began to look like the crotch I used to know, the patrol point man stepped into a punji pit. The pit measured approximately 2'x2'x2' deep. The squad leader told me to hang tight until they had him freed. If the pit had been booby trapped with a grenade, it would have blown his foot off. This pit was full of bamboo spikes covered with human feces. The Medevac chopper was called to airlift him to the NSA (Naval Support Activity) hospital in Da Nang. A point man's average life expectancy was a week to ten days. It was a dangerous volunteer occupation.

There were a lot of do(s) and don't(s) to remember. Actually, more don't(s) than do(s). Don't run into the crosshairs of a scope. Don't become predictable. Don't walk too close together. Don't always look for the easiest path; and the list went on and on.

My "down time" consisted of cleaning my equipment, writing letters to Cecelia and my folks, and getting to know my Marines. A jeep would be dispatched every day after the mine sweeping to the Battalion base for supplies and mail.

Mail call was the highlight of every day. It was the primary connection with "the world." I would keep the letters and read them again if I didn't get mail. The Marines in Alpha Company became my second family over the course of a few weeks. We would share what was happening at our homes. We began to know the parents, siblings, the girl friend or wife, our hopes, our aspirations and dreams.

Alpha Company had a detachment of armor called Amtraks. These "tracks" were named "The Addams Family" and were amphibious, however, we rarely used them in the water. They consisted of a driver and several support Marines. The heavy steel front would fold down for transporting small vehicles or troops. The tracks would sometimes lead a squad on patrol through a booby trap infested area. The small explosive devises were harmless to the tracks. The Amtrak would leave two wide track prints wherever it went.

The communication call sign for Alpha Company was Construe. Each patrol would pick up a call number and topographical map with a clear plastic cover at the Command Center. The route of the patrol would be traced on the clear plastic with a black grease pencil. There would be 4-6 check points along the route. The radioman would perform a radio check as the squad was leaving the perimeter.

"Alpha Command, this is Construe Alpha one. How do

you read? Over."

"Loud and clear Alpha one."

Construe Alpha One walked down to the T, crossed it and headed into the Red Zone.

"Watch your spacing men. Give yourself plenty of room," the squad leader reminded them.

They moved 30 yards apart on an Amtrak trail south along the east side of a thick row of bamboo. The point man stopped at a 90 degree confluence of bamboo intersecting the north/south bamboo.

"Papa Alpha, Construe Alpha One. Checkpoint one. "

"Roger that."

An Amtrak had punched through the thick bamboo intersection several days prior. The point man hesitated and then walked slowly between the tracks. Once on the far side, the remainder of the squad began to walk through the bamboo hedgerow. The fourth Marine followed the left track and disappeared. A huge explosion sent a plume of smoke and debris high into the air. Every Marine hit the ground. Most of them assumed a defensive prone position.

Within minutes the Command Center was shouting for a reactionary rescue squad. I grabbed my helmet, armored vest, cartridge belt, and medical bag as I sprinted with the reaction force through the front gate. The smoke of the explosion still hung in the air as we ran to the scene. The patrol Corpsman was moving from Marine to Marine checking their condition. I met the Doc after checking on the last uninjured Marines of the squad.

"I've called for the Medevac for two Marines next to the explosion."

We ran back to the site and tended to the wounded. The patrol Corpsman had put a large dressing on a through and through shoulder wound. I reinforced the soaked dressing and we moved both Marines to a makeshift landing zone (LZ). Two other Marines had superficial shrapnel wounds. Hearing the helicopter in the distance, we began looking for a missing Marine. As the chopper approached the LZ, we found pieces of David from Pennsylvania hanging high in the bamboo.

CHAPTER XI

Somber is not the word for the mood at Alpha Company. The entire garrison was devastated. Captain Sampson gathered us around his Command Center.

"Men, we have suffered an enormous loss. This is war and we still have a mission so get your head screwed on straight and don't let your guard down. Stay sharp. Talk to your Marines. Charlie gets no slack and its payback time. No ambushes will go out tonight. Dismissed."

David had stepped on an anti-tank mine planted by "Charlie" to destroy the Amtrak following the same path. I sat outside the Corpsman's tent the rest of the day. A quick shower erased the dust and mud but not the sight of my friend David.

Fuck this place. I still hadn't figured out why Uncle Sam had us in this shit hole. The jeep with the mail showed up just before lunch. Maybe a letter would cheer me up. No mail for Doc BJ but David got a letter and a package. It can be a cruel world. My mood sunk into despair. I skipped lunch and returned to the tent.

I had joined Alpha Company in May of 1967. I was 20 years old and a "cherry". The grunts called the green replacements "cherries". I guess it sounded better than "virgin". A couple months later, I was no longer a "cherry" and I had more time with Alpha Company than the other Corpsman. I listened to my mentors and somehow had survived. Walter Cronkite didn't need to butcher my name on the nightly news-- just yet.

I skipped the evening meal. David and I would sit in the mess tent discussing "round eyed" girls, muscle cars, and home. I knew the names of his family and he knew the names of mine.

We were family.

We were brothers.

I drifted asleep.

A Corpsman was shaking me. I sat up in the darkness. At first I thought I was on an ambush.

"What the---"

"Shh, pack up your gear. We're leaving on a mission at 2300 hours."

I picked my way through the night to Sergeant Green's platoon.

"Hey doc, you ready for this?"

"I don't know. Depends on what this is."

'The 5th Marines are south of the Bau Phong Thu river and will push everything north of them up against the river. They are the hammer. We will set up a block at the river to prevent an escape. We are the anvil."

"Who are we?"

"A platoon from Bravo, Charlie, and Delta companies will join our platoon along the river. We need to be there before daybreak."

At least I had gotten some sleep. All the territory between Alpha Company and the river was a free fire (red) zone. If it moves, waste it. We turned at the T, headed west for a klick (kilometer) then turned south toward the river. Two hours passed and the column stopped for several minutes. My mind wandered back to the events of the morning. It was obvious David had walked where he should not have walked. But, it was the easiest route. Easier than cutting and crawling through the bamboo carrying 50 pounds of gear. The "wait a minute" vines holding onto your canteen and ankles. Sweat running out from under your helmet into your eyes. Damned you David. Everyone who loves you is asking why.

My eyes began to sting about the time the night lit up with automatic M-16 and AK-47 fire. I stood watching as red and green tracers seem to collide a few feet from me. I hit the ground so hard it was like falling out of a tree. The Marine I had been following had grabbed my cartridge belt and slammed me into the dirt. As soon as it had started, the shooting stopped. Within 10 minutes we were again on our way to the river. As I passed the village well I noticed two Viet Cong dressed in black lying along the path. Their black pajamas were full of holes and an ace of spades protruded from their mouths. The company would get decks of cards containing 52 aces of spades. It became our death card to the gooks and it was attached to every dead body. I sincerely hoped they were the gooks who had planted the tank mine. The point element had surprised them. The only option was to kill them even though it meant exposing our position for miles.

Well before dawn the platoon reached Liberty Bridge. This structure had been built and rebuilt countless times as it was a vital link south toward the Central Highlands. The bridge remained under heavy security. By now I didn't have a clue what the hell we were doing besides walking around in the dark. In less than an hour we were deployed from Liberty Bridge southward to a piece of ground overlooking the village. Someone had figured out when the hammer approaches the anvil the gooks will attempt to escape out the sides. Two man listening posts were situated around the perimeter and a few of us took a nap.

As I ate my breakfast from a can, I surveyed the area. Alpha Company 1st platoon was spread out over a long, low berm. The river bordered the berm to the north. A large rice paddy flanked the village. We were ½ to ¾ mile west from the edge of the village. At first light the 5th Marines entered the village from the south. Constant small arms fire and explosions continued until early afternoon. The 5th Marines finally withdrew to regroup and recover their casualties. Meanwhile a tank from Liberty Bridge joined us. As enemy troops skirted the edge of the village, the tank would get their attention with a couple well placed rounds.

American military protocol in Vietnam had evolved into a dichotomy. What to do? A large Viet Cong force was embedded with mama-san and baby-san in the hamlet. Artillery and mortars would surly kill and wound innocent women and children. Air strikes were out of the question.

Let's make this war precise and nice. Find and kill the enemy while pacifying and coddling the nice guys, whoever the hell they were.

Precise. We don't want any collateral damage now, do we? Well, there was more than a little collateral damage when the bomb was dropped on Hiroshima.

And nice. Let's just tie pretty pink and blue ribbons in baby-san's hair while we win their hearts and minds. What a load of crap! This is what old men in suits think about while hiding in their Washington, D. C. office. Meanwhile, servicemen and women are dying. If Washington felt it was important to save America and its allies from communism, they should consider spending a few months with us. And while they are at it, bring some family members with them.

While the 5th Marines were busy with medical evacuation of their wounded and dead, a Company of Republic of Korea Marines (ROKs) provided a reactionary backup for the 5th. The ROKs entered the hamlet around 1400 hours. Continuous small arms and explosions blanketed the entire hamlet. At 1600 hours, the far north side of the hamlet was burning and the entire village was gone by 2000 hours. We dug in for another night. We knew we were under constant surveillance by the gooks. After nightfall, we made our defensive perimeter smaller and set claymore mines and trip flares where the perimeter used to be.

The night was uneventful. By mid-morning the platoon packed up and headed for Alpha Base. The Rice Paddy News was that the ROKs had eliminated everything breathing in the hamlet. Viet Cong, women, children, dogs, pigs, chickens, water buffalo, and then burned it down. No Korean red tape or spanking.

"Won't hafta worry bout dis dump no mo," said Frenchie, our M-60 Machine gunner.

"Reckon your right this time Frenchie. There weren't nothing in there I wanted anyway," St. John replied.

St. John, the L.A.W. man

CHAPTER XII

Captain Sampson surprised the entire company. It had been several days since the hammer and anvil operation. A jeep towing a two wheeled trailer made its way from Battalion Command out to Alpha Company. A corporal eased it to a stop in front of the Command Center. Two trucks filled with Marines followed the jeep through the main entry.

Alpha Marines began to gather wondering what was going down. The Captain walked into the crowd.

"Men, these Marines are providing security for us tonight. A trailer loaded with beer on ice is over there. Help yourself, you've earned it."

No whooping or hollering, just "hey, thanks boss." We

all hustled over to the trailer to find more than one brand. Wow! Black Label, Falstaff, Ballantine, and Schlitz. Hope the Charlie rats stay in their hole tonight. It's time for some relaxation.

Word came from Battalion the next morning we were part of a search and destroy operation north of Da Nang. The company bolstered its arsenal and manpower. A mortar crew and canine attachment from Battalion joined the fray. A fleet of Six-By trucks transported us to the mouth of a river valley flanked by elevated thick jungle. We followed the river that meandered along the valley floor. The temperature and humidity were both in the 90s. Military intelligence, which is an oxymoron, indicated a large force was preparing to attack the Da Nang air base. I spent the day passing out salt pills and ordering the Marines to drink plenty of water. In the middle of the afternoon, the dog handler carried his German shepherd to the river to cool him. I was always impressed with the canine units. The handler carried his equipment and provisions as well as taking care of the dog. The only breed I ever saw was the German shepherd. The dog had trouble recovering from the heat and was evacuated. The Captain decided to pitch camp and sent probing patrols out to snoop. Before sundown the Corpsmen made their "house calls" among the Marines, looking for signs of dehydration and dispensing malaria pills and salt tablets.

By daybreak, the enemy had infiltrated our encampment. The enemy was leeches the size of butter knives. Leeches thrive on blood and like nothing better than to find a nice warm armpit or groin during the night to call home.

"Doc, I got a problem," announced the Gunnery Sergeant. He dropped his pants and several dozen leeches were attached to his groin. The easiest way to attack leeches imbedded in the skin is to touch them with something hot.

"Are you going to just fucking stand there? Do something," yelled Gunny.

I looked at my fellow Corpsman. "I'll take the back and you take the front."

"No, you take the front and I"II take the back."

I thought the Gunny was going to explode. His blood pressure was rising and the leeches were merrily munching away.

"Okay, okay, step out of your britches and we'll get to work."

We each lit up a cigarette and touched a leech with the hot match. Each subsequent leech was touched with the hot end of the cigarette. Within minutes, Gunny's legs were red with blood. A leech has an anticoagulant so the blood doesn't clot while they are gorging. We called for another Corpsman to bring us large battle dressings. With the leeches off and diapered up with dressings, Gunny growled.

"You expect me to fight with this covering my ass? I don't think so."

"Sit down and relax Gunny. We need to see if anyone else is donating blood."

Nearly everyone had a few leeches but they took a cue from us and burned them off.

We returned to Gunny and his dressing was saturated. Word had spread around the camp that Gunny wore diapers and he snarled at anyone looking at him. It was decided to have Gunny clean himself up at the river. After he dried, we covered the leech marks with antibiotic ointment and had him wear a battle dressing under his pants and he would be evaluated in 12 hours.

The Corpsmen had a meeting to figure out how we were going to deal with this unconventional enemy. Since the unit was staying at the campsite for at least another day, the Corpsmen told all the Marines to save the small salt packets found in their C-rations. We emptied a couple jars of salt tablets and crushed them. Everyone was ordered to open and sleep on their rain poncho with salt sprinkled within the outer edges. The salt would sting the moist leeches. We still had some leech problems but it was minimal.

One of the probe patrols hit the jackpot. They had found an elevated lookout that was not covered by triple canopy jungle. Instead of cutting their way through low visibility jungle, they were able to glass the surrounding high ground and river valley from a vantage point. They had spotted activity on the river further up the valley and monitored the movement of sampans and personnel.

"Papa 1, this is Construe Alpha two."

"Go ahead two."

"We have a visual on Victor Charlie. Over."

"Roger that. Hang on. Six-Actual wants your transmit."

The Captain took the handset.

"How many and what's their position. Over."

"We spotted the first sampan about 20 minutes ago. They're loaded and riding low in the water and they just keep coming. Must be at least three or more. Over."

"Troops, how many troops? Over."

"Don't rightly know but there must be a staging area up the river a piece. Over."

"What's your position? Over."

"Check point three. Over."

"Stay put and wait for my come back. Out."

The Captain was back on the horn in minutes.

"Da Nang is scrambling some Phantoms. They are instructed to fly down the middle of the valley to cover the river and the lateral tree lines. When they enter the valley, I want you to fire a white phosphorous marker. Here is their frequency. Dial it up and give them directions. Over."

"Roger that."

We were close enough to the Da Nang air strip to hear jets arriving and leaving on their missions. Within minutes the Captain gave the word. "Mark it."

The White Phosphorous round arced out over the steep hillside and disappeared into the jungle. After what seemed like an eternity, wisps of white smoke appeared over the canopy. Sampans were being pulled into the cover along the river banks. Three Phantoms abreast entered the valley.

"The mark is left of the river. Your target is 500 meters north. Over."

"Roger that."

The middle Phantom roared by and opened up with his cannons straight down the river. Seconds later the other two Phantoms dropped half their load of bombs. As they ascended out of the valley, two more Phantoms dropped napalm 50 and 100 yards from each side of the river. Secondary explosions erupted sending fire and smoke into the sky.

The probe patrol was hustling back to the encampment. The scattering gooks would be looking for the source of the white phosphorous also known as Willie Peter or WP. Time to di di mau. The patrol nearly got shot as it entered the encampment's fire zone. Nervous fingers on triggers is a dangerous thing.

The air strike continued for nearly an hour. Smoke hung over the high ridges overlooking the valley. The Captain tightened up the perimeter and set out every claymore mine. Everyone had a delicious warm C-ration dinner before nightfall. No fire or lights were allowed after dark.

As I consumed my can of beans & weenies, I wondered why we were still camping. It was not for me to say, but nobody's saying I can't wonder. Then it dawned on me. The Generals sitting in the relative safety of 1st Marine Division Headquarters in Da Nang needed an enemy body count. The major television networks would report the enemy losses which were huge compared to the 20 or so American losses. It must have made the fat cats in Washington, D. C. feel a little better about the war.

It was SOP (Standard Operating Procedure) to clean up the debris before we abandoned an area. Nothing was to be left behind that the gooks could use as booby traps. Everything that was burnable was put into a large pile. The fire was at its peak when a "bang" was followed by a painful scream. Startled Marines assumed defensive positions and Corpsmen watched as one Marine was "dancing" around the fire. In the process of gathering C-ration cardboard to burn, a small tin of peanut butter had been left in one of the boxes. Exploding, it sent hot peanut oil and butter airborne. The Marine finally stopped "dancing." His blisters were minor and treated amid good natured banter from his buddies.

In from the mine sweep covered in dirt.

After the shower.

5 Star Accommodations

CHAPTER XIII

We broke camp the next morning and headed for Da Nang. The stand down was unexpected and speculation ran rampant. Division Headquarters ordered the operation toward a hotbed of Viet Cong activity just north of the Da Nang airbase. "Charlie" would routinely infiltrate Monkey Mountain to harass the base with sniper and mortar fire. When the military Brass had enough, they would send in the troops to wipe it clean. Then the troops would leave and the gooks would return. Hmmm, some more military intelligence?

Back at Alpha base, I again was on a rotation. Day patrols, night ambushes, and the mine sweeping team on my day off was the routine. The floor of our Corpsman tent was made of 105mm artillery boxes filled with sand and placed side by side and end to end. In the event of a heavy rain, we were not living in mud. The scraps from C-rations and an occasional treat of goodies from home would find their way between the cracks.

I awoke from a restful sleep just before dawn with a heaviness on my chest. Slowly opening my eyes I looked straight into the face of a rat the size of a muskrat. The commotion made by me bailing out of the tent woke the other Corpsmen who thought we were under attack. Hence forth, there was no eating food in the tent.

Less than a week later, I developed a 103 plus degree temperature. I was transported to the BAS (Battalion Aid Station) for evaluation. On my way into the BAS I passed out cold. I woke up on a cot with the shakes and an IV in my left arm. Getting an infusion is like drinking a 12 pack of beer in that I had to urinate on a regular basis. A BAS Corpsman helped me out to the piss tube holding the IV bag of fluid in his other hand. Lights out again. My temperature had spiked well over 104 degrees. When I woke up, the Battalion Surgeon decided to send me into Da Nang for treatment. My FUO (fever of unknown origin) broke after three days and I was sent back to Battalion. Nobody could seem to figure out what had caused the fever but it was gone. Good enough, at least for now.

During this time, I couldn't get David out of my head. This was the first big loss of my life and I was overwhelmed by the emotional pain. I became filled with anger bordering on rage. Melancholy turned to depression. On my ride out to Alpha Base, I decided to not make friends with "my" Marines. I didn't need, nor did I want to know about their family back in "the world", their wives or sweethearts, their hopes and aspirations. Camaraderie has its consequences. If I were to survive emotionally, I decided to build an emotional wall. I would be friendly but not friends. It was simply a matter of self-preservation. This created an unintended problem which followed me around for the better part of my life. It is near impossible to hit the off switch. Now I realized what the grunts meant by becoming "hard."

Returning to Alpha Base, I found a couple new additions to the company. A sniper unit commanded by famed Marine Corps sniper Carlos Hathcock (white feather) had been deployed to Hill 55, the 1st Battalion's base. One of his snipers was using Alpha Base as an area of operation. I don't know if he was antisocial or just a mysterious sort of guy. He never carried on a conversation about his missions. We all knew he was hunting the sniper(s) that were hunting us. He did have a peculiar habit, however, of bringing "pets" back to the base. The first "pet" was a monkey, then a puppy followed by an ocelot cat that had been blinded probably by collateral damage. The last straw was two immature cobras that he would tease so they would stand and open their hood.

Enter Captain Sampson. "We're not running a fucking zoo here so get rid of that shit. NOW."

They all disappeared except the puppy which was kept as an Alpha Company mascot.

The other addition was a team of German Shepherd guard dogs named Mutsu and Beju. They were trained to kill. I was introduced to them as I stood over a piss tube in the middle of a dark night. It is difficult hitting a piss tube on a starless night. With two dogs growling and glaring at my crotch urinating didn't matter.

Anyway, the gooks had stepped up their mine planting and the company responded by positioning the night ambushes near the road. A guard dog became part of the ambush site. The results were immediate. Instead of having two Marines on watch, one Marine would monitor the radio and watch the dog. When the dogs ears went up and it looked in the direction of the threat, the ambush went on alert. Illumination flares would expose hints of the black pajama clad VC planting mines in the road. The mortar crew at Alpha Command would throw up the magnesium flare. After a pause, the Marine on the radio would key his handset twice and the next mortars were   live rounds landing on or close to the dinks. Battalion Command SOP (Standard Operating Procedure) was to request a fire mission from Battalion Headquarters. Headquarters wanted to know the what, where, and why for mortars or artillery. By the time all that nonsense had been shared, there was no need for a fire mission. Our Company Commander would approve the fire mission without prior authorization. After all, it was his Marines' asses on the line. He would explain to Battalion the what, where, and why after the fact. Battalion Headquarters wasn't fond of his decisions but we loved him. He had our back.

Returning from a mine sweeping gig, I grabbed my mess kit and was heading for breakfast when word came down from the communication center a four man recon team was in trouble. A reaction squad and Amtrak headed for the main gate where it stopped.

"We need a Corpsman. Get a Corpsman over here pronto."

Racing back to the tent, I threw the mess kit on my cot while grabbing my medical bag and rifle. We rode the

Amtrak over the road into "Indian country". Plowing through anything that got in the way, we finally hooked up with the team. Two members were guarding the site while one member was hunched over the wounded Marine. I jumped off the Amtrak while the reaction squad fanned out. The tending Marine was pressing a t-shirt on the upper leg of the downed Marine.

"Good to see you Doc. You need to do something fast. A sniper got him."

The Marine was semi-conscious from hemorrhagic shock. A couple Marines rolled him on his side which exposed a gapping exit wound that was bleeding profusely. I applied a tourniquet and battle dressings on the entry and exit wounds.

"We gotta get him outta here. GO, GO!"

Once inside the Amtrak, I used my K-bar knife to cut the tape that held the plasma canister on the strap of my medical bag. I told a Marine to open the plasma as I retrieved the IV kit from my bag. The door to the Amtrak had closed and we were bouncing over rice paddy dikes at maximum speed.

"Doc, the driver wants to know if he should call for a chopper."

"Tell him to head for the BAS. The chopper can meet us there."

I threw the IV tubing to the Marine and told him to puncture the plasma bottle with the sharp end and fill the tubing. Meanwhile, I had a second Marine squeeze the upper arm with both hands as I searched in the darkness for a vein. The IV needles were long stainless steel with a large bore so the transfusion was fast.

Damn it, I couldn't see because of the dark interior of the Amtrak and I couldn't feel the vein on the inside of his elbow. The wounded Marine was not responding and his pulse was becoming weaker. I slipped the needle under the skin and eased it forward. I can't let this Marine die. I could almost hear Captain Crunch. "The Marines will watch over you because their very life may be in your hands."

The needle produced nothing.

"God damn it, will someone give me some fucking light," I screamed over the roar of the Amtrak engine.

Simultaneously, the front of the Amtrak opened. The Battalion surgeon and his Corpsmen started an IV in his opposite arm and opened the plasma full throttle. By the time the medevac chopper arrived, the Marine was on his third plasma and had started to respond.

"Doc, here's your rifle. You left it back at the river."

Losing a rifle was a major screw up. I returned it to Sergeant Green. Besides, if we were getting our ass kicked, there would probably be a spare rifle somewhere.

Doubt again flooded over me. Was I truly prepared for the responsibility inherent with being called a Hospital Corpsman? Had I been adequately trained for every possibility? Will this brave Marine who entrusted his life to me survive? I didn't have the answers. Within a week, the word was that he had been airlifted to the Naval Hospital in Japan. The Battalion surgeon told me the Marine had damage to his femoral artery and would have died within minutes without the compress, tourniquet and pressure dressings. That gave me a shot of confidence but didn't totally erase some of my doubts.

Several days later, I joined the patrol next to the river that flanked the Battalion Base. As we slowly walked along a rice paddy dike, we came under fire from the opposite river bank. There was nowhere to go but into the rice paddy.

As we laid in the water and mud a Lieutenant gave the order to charge the tree line. Sergeant Lambert asked him if he was a fucking idiot and called in air support. The Marine Corps phantom jet pilot asked for a mark. The white phosphorus smoke hit the bank 100 meters east of the target. If it was fired on the target, the target would move. Our radioman relayed the position to the pilot as we hunkered down in the mud. The phantom approached from behind us and released two napalm canisters. Napalm canisters tumble. Rolling over us, we could almost read the writing on the canisters. The tree line was engulfed in a huge fire storm. The threat had been fried.

Warm beer

CHAPTER XIV

October, 1967

Battalion was directed to relocate to Hill 10 which sat within the rice paddies at the mouth of the second leg of the Ho Chi Mein trail. The Ho Chi Mein trail began at the DMZ (Demilitarized Zone) and followed the Laotian/Cambodian border the entire length of Viet Nam with spurs turning inland at strategic locations. Alpha Company occupied a small pimple of a hill one kilometer north of Hill 10. Captain Sampson had been promoted and was now part of 1st Marine Division staff. Our new Commanding Officer was totally impressed with himself. He treated the Company as if it were still in basic training. Scuttlebutt was that he had had a cushy position at Division Headquarters but wasn't a team player so they sent him and his attitude out to us. Thank you very fucking much!

The pimple sat smack dab in the middle of a free fire zone. No civilians, just gooks trying to kill us. We found out what it feels like to be the bait. The only thing that would save our ass if the VC and NVA (North Vietnamese army) decided to eliminate us were air strikes and artillery. The Corpsmen assisted the Marines filling hundreds of sand bags and fashioned a clinic with sleeping quarters. I put an eight by eleven inch picture of Cecelia next to my cot. I would write often unless we were on a search and destroy mission. My letters to her and to my family were sugar-coated. No sense in sharing the gory details.

The daily routine resembled the previous Alpha Base. Daily patrols and night ambushes along with extending the clearing outside the perimeter so the gooks couldn't sneak up on us. The one big difference was the prick Captain. Ambushes would look forward to the stand down after returning from a night in the jungle. Light up a cigarette, enjoy a warm breakfast, and catch up on some shut-eye.

Not in the Captain's world. The smoking lamp was not lit until he decided it was lit. No breakfast allowed until the ambush put on clean clothes and fell in for physical fitness exercise. Anyone not following his rules was subject to a warning and then a demotion. Complaining only resulted in added harassment. Moral plummeted.

Pissing the troops off in a combat zone has a tendency to result in serious   consequences.

Marines died confronting the enemy.

Occasionally, Marines died as a result of friendly fire.

Pricks sometimes met their demise from "unfriendly" fire.

The Captain had become a gigantic boil on our ass. Talk began circulating about adjusting his attitude.

"I say we frag the bastard."

The plan was to seize the opportunity when the gooks probed our perimeter which happened periodically. Because the Captain was chicken shit, he would always hide in his bunker. A fragmentation grenade would mysteriously find its way into his bunker. There's a cure for everything.

The Sergeant came up with an option. When the Captain was making his daily inspection of the numerous perimeter bunkers, a grenade was placed on top of his clothes inside his foot locker. He was a prick but probably not a stupid prick. Hopefully the grenade would get the point across.

The change was instant and dramatic. He had no choice. Division didn't want him back and the writing was on the wall. The company returned to normal; a disciplined fighting machine.

A Marine Lieutenant fresh from the war college joined our Company. As we were preparing to go out on our daily patrol, he walked up to Sergeant Green and gave him a snappy salute the sergeant did not return.

"I'm going with you this morning Sarge."

"Great, but not dressed like that, sir."

"What do you mean?"

"First off, get rid of the Lieutenant bars on your helmet and collar."

"How is anyone going to know who I am?"

"No disrespect sir, but nobody really cares who you are. And get rid of those new starched clothes. Put on some well used camo. You stick out like a sore thumb and I don't want you getting any of my men killed. Oh, and by the way, we don't salute out here. The gooks would just love to pop an officer."

The squad watched the exchange and grinned as the "Lieut" disappeared. As we zigzagged through the barbed wire, the Lieutenant rejoined the patrol. In the long run, he became a very good Marine Officer. He lost his arrogance, listened to the veteran Marines and survived.

We moved into the thick overgrowth and slowly made our way to check point one. The first check point was an ancient pagoda temple. It had been abandoned and was covered with vines. An hour later we reached check point two. Our shirts were soaked from sweat. I passed out salt pills while checking for signs of dehydration. As we were approaching check point three, the squad stopped. The point man was suspicious of an arched structure. He carefully surveyed the structure and surrounding vines and vegetation. Satisfied it presented no apparent danger, he walked step at a time through the opening. Five more yards and the explosion blasted Martinez. Nobody yelled "Corpsman up." It was obvious Martinez had been injured. I found him sitting and holding his left hand. His camo trousers had been riddled by shrapnel. An assessment of his mangled hand revealed several missing fingers including part of his thumb. The radial artery was pumping out blood with every heartbeat. As the radioman called for the medevac, I applied a medium battle dressing and wrapped it tight with gauze strips. I cut each trouser leg up to the hips. Multiple puncture wounds were oozing. With no apparent arterial damage, I injected 10 grains of morphine into his upper thigh. I was nearly finished applying wraps to each leg when the medevac chopper approached the LZ (Landing Zone). I reinforced the dressing on his left hand and moved him through the downdraft of the chopper.

"You're gonna be alright," I yelled above the din of the landing chopper. "You got a million dollar wound."

A "million dollar wound" was severe enough to put the Marine out of action and a one way ticket to "the world". Martinez tried to give me a thumbs. Instead he gave me a pained smile, and he was gone.

Battalion Command decided to send us a gook called a Kit Carson scout. A Kit Carson scout was typically a Viet Cong who had decided to defect to the American Armed Forces. One of the propaganda programs was to drop leaflets from aircraft. The leaflets granted the Viet Cong amnesty if they joined the American cause. They would be interrogated by the "chieu hoi" interrogators. The interrogators would decide if they were sincere and trustworthy. Perfect. Just perfect. Graduating from the chieu hoi program didn't mean they were at the top of their class. Kit Carson scouts traveled with squads and were used as an interpreter of radio transmissions, captured documents and face to face encounters. They could also warn the Marines of impending enemy contact. But would they? Our scout was allowed to carry a pistol. None of the Marines trusted him. They viewed him as a potential threat inside our wire.

Dell Allen

Hot!

Medevac

CHAPTER XV

For some unknown reason the bait wasn't devoured by the Viet Cong. Alpha Company was ordered to abandon the pimple and was moved closer to tighten up the defensive cordon protecting the Da Nang air base. At the same time, I was transferred to the Battalion Aid Station. I had spent nearly eight months with my Marines in Alpha Company. Four months left of my "senior class trip" to Vietnam. Battalion was support for the Companies operating on the periphery. I joined the BAS medical crew which was responsible for the overall health of the Battalion. As always, Marines with venereal puss dripping out of their dicks would wait in line every morning at the sick bay for their diet of penicillin.

Casualties of war. Sorry buddy, no Purple Heart for you.

Dr. Hines from Texas was the Battalion Surgeon. The Corpsmen put their heads together and came up with what seemed like a common sense solution. We would use some of our penicillin to clean up the prostitutes and only allow infection free Marines to patronize them. The Battalion surgeon was intrigued by the idea. One of the Marines we were treating decided to write his mama with the news. His mama contacted her Congressman and the Congressman contacted the General. The General's liaison paid a visit to our Battalion Surgeon who denied any knowledge of the complaint.

At the VD (Venereal Disease) lineup the next day the senior corpsman made an announcement.

"One of you is most likely responsible for the visit and reprimand we received from Headquarters yesterday. Your mama would probably enjoy grandchildren someday. Personally, I hope your dick rots off."

The sanitation and preventive medicine of the Battalion was part of the medical crew's inspection. Corporal Corillio, an Italian Marine from New York City, volunteered to be the sanitation engineer. His daily duties made him exempt from both patrols and ambushes. He made sure the piss tubes were draining well and he checked the barrels in the shitters on a daily basis. Each shitter was two seated. A large barrel was cut in half and a half barrel was placed under each seat. When the barrels were half full, he would open the back access door, pull the barrel out and burn it with a couple gallons of diesel fuel. Making the rounds, he would return to the first barrels which were no longer hot and place them back in the shitter. When the barrels were too full to burn, he would load them on a mule (military ATV), drive outside the gate, and dump them into a deep trench.

"What did you do in the war Daddy?"

"Well let me tell you son, I had to put up with a lot of shit."

The gooks had a different system. Each morning the villagers would wade into the rice paddy, pull up their pajama leg and squat. They would jabber back and forth while adding to the piss and shit. I didn't realized that taking a dump could be a social event.

We never encountered men, or boys for that matter over the age of ten, while patrolling the hamlets in our (AO) area of operation. Younger children would gather around us begging for anything we would give them. They really enjoyed Juicy Fruit gum. Sometimes we would slip them a "fizzy" (a flavored tablet that bubbled like an Alka Selzer when wet). They would spit it out and say, "you numba ten." Numba ten meant you were bad. Numba one meant you were good. When the children did not show, we knew the Viet Cong were close by. I slowly became empathetic toward the average Vietnamese who were just trying to raise their family and worked to provide basic meager provisions for them. They were not interested in Communism or Democracy. They just wanted to be left alone. The Viet Cong would demand information from the papa-san or tell him to set mines. If he refused, they would kill his family. If we caught him we would either kill him or at the very least detain him.

In an attempt to become a good neighbor to the villagers bordering our combat base, a detail of Marines and Corpsmen were sent periodically into the hamlet on a MEDCAP program. The Corpsmen would provide villagers with treatment of various wounds and illnesses while the

Marines set up security. I encountered a four year old boy with a scalp infection. The mama-son had covered the wound with water buffalo dung which kept flies from laying eggs in the infection. I soaked the dung off and replaced it with an antibiotic gauze soaked in antibiotic ointment. The next week I made a follow-up visit to find the gauze had been replaced with the freshest dung available.

The Vietnamese called the Corpsmen Bac si which meant doctor. Their idea of medical intervention was very foreign to western civilization. Much of their remedies were herbs and ancient concoctions. Dental care didn't exist, at least not in the rural areas of the country. Dental pain was treated with betel nut which had an anesthetic affect, both topically and systemic. Chewing betel nut produced a red saliva which eventually turned their teeth black. During one MEDCAP we noticed a much taller Vietnamese woman with beautiful facial features and long black hair. She was most likely a product of the French occupation of Vietnam.

"Hey, mama-san, you numba one!"

She turned and smiled at us with a mouthful of black teeth.

Well, maybe numba eight!

On another occasion, we found a young girl with life threatening wounds. I held her in my lap as a Marine corporal drove the jeep into Da Nang. We stopped at a German Hospital ship in the Da Nang harbor whose mission was to provide humanitarian medical treatment. I carried the girl on board and passed her to a German nurse in a uniform so white she looked like an angel. An angel I tell you, with round eyes! The corporal and I were covered in dust from our trip. A German with coal black hair and beard asked if we would like a beer. We each devoured three of the coldest brew we had had in months. By the time we passed the last guard shack leaving Da Nang it was dusk. The corporal drove at breakneck speed as I had the rifle on full automatic. Returning to base, I popped a green flare to indicate a "friendly" was approaching the front gate. The Battlion Colonel saved the ass chewing for the next day. We deserved it but it was worth it.

One half mile down the main road from the Battalion was a small Combined Action Platoon base consisting of ARVN (army of republic of Vietnam) soldiers along with American advisors. The ARVNs were good fighters when they had no choice. A call came from them into the Battalion Command Communication Center shortly after midnight. They were in imminent danger of being overrun and were being hit hard with small arms fire and rocket propelled grenades (RPGs).

I joined the reactionary force escorted by a tank responding to their call for help. Hardcore Viet Cong had set us up. They were not stupid. They knew we would get the call and come racing down the road. Running along the right rear corner of the tank, we were ambushed from both sides of the road. An RPG hit the left side of the tank turret next to the Marine manning the 30 caliber machine gun. Moisture hit me in the face as I ducked. All hell was breaking loose. The Marines had their M-16s on "rock-n-roll" spraying the road ditches with a hail of bullets. The darkness was full of red and green tracers and sparks from exploding grenades. One Marine climbed on the tank while throwing a full clip into his rifle.

"Corpsman up," he yelled.

I tried to crawl up the rear of the moving tank. Feeling for a handhold, I grabbed a handful of air and landed face down in the road. Again hearing a call for a Corpsman, I sprinted to the tank and launched myself up on the rear of the tank. I crawled to the machine gunner lying on the turret. I put my ear to his face. Not hearing any breaths, I search for his carotid pulse and it wasn't there. The grenade had destroyed the side of his head and carotid artery.

The intensity of the ambush eventually subsided to an occasional burst of gun fire. The tank did a 180 turn and stopped. Marines were loading wounded comrades on the tank.

"Doc, you need me to call for a medevac?"

"No, get this damned thing moving. We need to get back to the BAS."

The progress of the tank became slower and slower. Just inside the front gate it settled to a stop. What the hell? The driver was slumped over. Trying not to slip off the tank, I helped pull the driver out of his seat while another Marine hit the gas. Pulling up in front of the BAS, every Corpsman and the Battalion surgeon carried the wounded down into the treatment bunker. The tank driver had a hole just beneath his left clavicle. As a team of Corpsmen were attempting to start an IV, another Marine cried out.

"Help me. Damn it, someone please help me."

I looked around and every Corpsman was busy trying to save Marines. I opened the Marine's armored vest and shirt. Blood was gushing out of a wound between his ribs just below his armpit. I ripped open an IV kit and grabbed for a bottle of plasma. When I looked back at him, his eyes were glazed and he had stopped breathing.

"Jesus doc, are you hit?"

My face and arms were covered with dried blood, and tissue clung to my armored jacket.

"I don't think so," I mumbled.

The tank still stood in front of the BAS when the sun peeked over the eastern horizon. The blood on the tank had dried and turned black. It was a reminder of the night of horrors. What was left of the reactionary squad returned to the base. A medevac chopper transported the wounded to Da Nang in the pre-dawn hours. A second chopper took the dead to Graves Registration in Da Nang at daybreak. The BAS medical team was exhausted but the war didn't care. We canceled sick call for the morning and cleaned up the carnage in the treatment bunker.

By mid-morning, I was standing under a cool shower provided by a metal tank atop a wooden frame. The tank was filled with water each morning and the sun warmed the water throughout the day. A sharp pain on the top of my right index finger got my attention as I rubbed my left hand over it. Close inspection revealed a thin metal shard which I removed and tossed aside. Purple Heart? It was a fleeting thought. The Marines who lost their lives will be awarded a Purple Heart post humorously while I wore a Purple Heart for a sliver. I couldn't live with that. Besides, a military representative would visit my parents with news that I had been wounded in action. Not going to happen!

If only the soap and water would wash away the gut wrenching decision of treating Marines who had a chance to live while the survival of others was marginal at best.

Now I lay me down to sleep.

I pray the Lord my soul to keep.

If I should die before I wake.

I pray the Lord my soul to take.

God bless Daddy, Mommy, Sister, and Brother.

Amen.

Raised within a family who faithfully attended church every Sunday, I was baptized and confirmed in the Christian faith. I attended Sunday school, Tuesday school, Vacation Bible School, and sang in the choir at the Good Shepard Lutheran Church.

I am sure my parents prayed for me every night. I do not recall praying during my time in Vietnam and I don't know exactly why. Maybe it was "thy will be done on earth as it is in heaven."   Why would the Good Shepard allow such brutal carnage? Maybe my faith was being put to the test.

CHAPTER XVI

The troops in Vietnam were given a respite from the war by traveling to select destinations for five days. This was called R & R (rest & relaxation) or as the troops called it, I & I (intoxication & intercourse). Hawaii was reserved for married personnel if they hadn't received a "Dear John" letter.

The guys who were servicing the wives and girlfriends back home were called "Jody." I was told to apply for R & R and the list included Tokyo, Bangkok, Taipei, Manilla and Australia. Just when I thought I might see the land down under, I found out the officers were taking all the available accommodations. Any place for a week was better than this hell hole.

I hadn't heard from Cecelia in a couple months. When I returned from Tokyo, I wrote her a long letter as I had a suspicion our time apart wasn't going well. A week later she wrote to say things were not going to work out between us.

That night I sat on the sandbags surrounding my little corner of an uncertain world and tried to make some sense of the unknown. I did know that she had been a part of my will to survive. The next morning, I removed her picture from over my cot. I stored it in my foot locker----just in case.

The Bob Hope Christmas show was entertaining the troops in Southeast Asia and Da Nang was one of his stops. My father had attended the Bob Hope show during WWII. The 1st Marine Division wanted actual combat troops to occupy the first ten rows of the show so I asked Dr. Hines for permission to be part of the audience. He said he would consider my request. I was seriously in need of a moral boost.

Each morning the Corpsman would fall in formation in the front of the BAS for a briefing by the chief Corpsman. Dr. Hines made a cameo appearance and selected me and another Corpsman to attend the Christmas show in Da Nang. Bob Hope was great and a lot of laughs, Les Brown and his band of renown was---yawn, but Raquel Welch— well now! As she danced in the fur bikini made famous in her movie, she asked for a dance partner. The first two rows joined her.

Christmas arrived right on schedule on December 25th. Of course, the clinic was not closed for the Holiday. One of the Corpsman fashioned a sign he hung by the penicillin administration line; MERRY SYPHILIS AND A CLAPPY NEW YEAR.

Most of the Corpsmen had received "care packages" from home. My mother had sent a metal coffee can packed with home-made chocolate chip cookies which I shared with my tent mates. Corpsman Reed from Texas received a small tinfoil Christmas tree which was mounted on a foot locker. Dr. Hines brought up a ham and several bottles of champagne. We listened to and sang Christmas carols on a Pioneer recorder, drank champagne, and forgot about the war for a few hours.

I woke up out of a sound sleep to the scream of rockets passing over the tent. Stepping into my boots I grabbed my helmet, medical bag and flak jacket. Running out the front door with the other Corpsmen, I headed for the heavily sand-bagged BAS treatment bunker. Another rocket swooshed in. MERRY CHRISTMAS! Three of us hit the ground. The rocket passed over us and landed on the roof of the Communication bunker. Corpsman Sweatz and I scrambled to our feet and ran to the smoking ruins. The rocket had partially penetrated the sandbagged roof. We found the Marines on duty with non-life-threatening wounds. Smoke inhalation and a few ruptured ear drums.

The gooks had a small market outside the front gate of the base. They would arrive every morning to set up shop. They sold black market cokes, Ho Chi Mein sandals, souvenirs, and a variety of crafts. There was also a barber who cut hair with a manual clipper and shaved with a straight edge razor. I was always amazed at the Marines who would allow him to shave their necks and face. Not this farm boy! The gooks would count the steps a Marine made between the Communication bunker and the market. When they left the market for the day, they would count their steps from the market to the rocket launching site. BULLS EYE!

The Commanding Officer of 1st Battalion announced a General from Division was planning to grace us with his presence for an award ceremony. Well, la de fucking da. Those who were not on duty were ordered to wear clean camos and attend.

The General arrived on a Huey helicopter and was met by the Colonel amidst banners flying in the breeze. The recipients were in formation at full attention. Most of the presentations were purple hearts for being wounded in action with a bronze star or two. Special recognition was given to the reactionary squad for the Combined Action Platoon.

"Hey Doc, you were on that squad," whispered Corpsman Butterfield.

"Yah, I was."

"This is a bunch of bullshit. And why is Gibbs getting a purple heart?"

"Beats the hell outa me. I don't know."

I decided to talk to Dr. Hines about the awards ceremony. He informed me that the Lieutenant who led the reactionary team reported that there was no Corpsman present when he was wounded in the foot. He was awarded a purple heart and a bronze star for bravery. A Hospital Corpsman received a purple heart for skinning his elbow when he dove to the ground during the rocket attack. I wonder what the award citations really read. Medals on a uniform look nice. Sometimes they are not worth the price of a cup of coffee.

CHAPTER XVII

TET, 1968

The Vietnamese celebrate TET, the Lunar New Year.

To honor their holiday, a truce was called. Is this a war or a football game? What the hell is with a time out? Well, a time out is usually called when a team needs to regroup and discuss their next plan of attack. What did Captain Crunch say about shit for brains?

The NVA began the siege on the Provincial Capital of Hue (pronounced Way) on January 31, 1968. A company of Marines moved north on Hwy 1 to provide security and ran into a hornet's nest. Our Battalion was put on alert and advised we would be moved north on a moment's notice. This becomes a domino effect. Who will take our place defending the Da Nang Air Base? And who would take the place of the Marines replacing us? Although we had packed our bags, it seemed a remote possibility.

While the American war machine was preparing for a little slack, the NVA and Viet Cong had equipped themselves for coordinated strategic attacks from the DMZ (demilitarized zone) in the north to the Delta in the south. Rules of War prohibited us from breaking the TET truce by shooting at the enemy. That is, unless we were shot at first.

So, let's make sure we all understand. We can only return fire if they shoot at us--- and miss? Then, and only then, can we plead self-defense. Now, that's just brilliant! Who the hell came up with these rules of engagement? I am quite certain it wasn't the guys busting their ass in the rice paddies and jungles.

The Gunnery Sergeant who had donated a unit of blood to the leeches showed up at the BAS morning muster. After rollcall and assignments were completed, the Chief Corpsman announced "Gunny" was taking two Corpsmen at a time to the rifle range outside the front gate. It had occurred to him that the "squids" were probably a little rusty in basic weaponry. Collectively, we had not fired a round during our tour of duty and, with TET approaching, that could very well change.

Hospital Corpsman Reed and I were instructed to "break down" our .45 cal. Pistol. I popped the clip and opened the breach ensuring there was no round in the chamber. I laid the pistol and clip on the bed of the "mule" and stepped back. Reed laid all the pieces of his pistol next to mine.

"Doc, have you had your 45 out of the holster since the day it was issued?"

Gunny was a career no nonsense Marine who enjoyed carrying non-issued weapons. His favorite was a short barreled shot gun with buckshot. He was a ballistics genius and could disassemble and assemble anything blindfolded.

I heard he had been Gunnery Sergeant many times.

"No Gunny, I haven't."

"Well Doc, Corpsman Reed seems to have it figured out, hasn't he?"

"I guess so Gunny, but he's from Texas."

We spent nearly a half hour taking them apart and putting them back together. Satisfied we had passed that test, we each loaded several clips and assumed a standing position 30 yards from paper targets. Reed emptied his first clip and hit all but one. Meanwhile I hit only one. In the second round, Reed put all his rounds on the target. Again, I hit one. Gunny walked over and picked up my last clip.

"I'm just checking to see if you're using live rounds."

Gunny tossed me the clip and put me at the 20 yard marker where I ripped the edge off the target with two rounds. Gunny is now losing his patience.

"What the fuck are you doing? Are you closing your eyes? I seriously doubt you could hit a bull in the ass with a shovel."

On a whim, Reed and I traded pistols and I filled the target with every round while Reed's last round found the paper. Gunny confiscated my .45, gave it a critical look and grumbled.

"Piece of shit. Musta been made by the lowest bidder."

A small river meandered to the north of the Battalion base. The rubble from an old French outpost overlooked the river. BAS Corpsmen were now on a patrol/ambush rotation. Leaving the base well after nightfall, the ambush settled in at the outpost. With the 0300 to 0500 watch I would get four to five hours of sleep and I didn't waste any time.

Again, I was jolted awake by the sound of rockets. This

was not an instant replay. I rolled over on my stomach as small arms fire danced around us. Projectiles passing within inches sound like Rice Krispies. They snap and crackle. You don't want to hear the pop.

"Corpsman! Doc, get over here."

I crawled to the edge of the outpost while Frenchie blazed away with his M-60 machine gun on his hip Rambo style. In the sporadic light of the rocket flashes, I found Danny lying on his back.

"Danny, Danny," I yelled as I shook him.

He didn't answer. His carotid pulse was weak and he was gasping for air. I lifted his jaw forward to open his airway with no success. Agonal breathing proceeded to apnea. I leaned over him, pinched his nose, and gave him a couple quick breaths. I placed my ear next to his mouth. Nothing. His carotid pulse had disappeared.

The ambush and the Battalion were firing a wall of lead at the river bank. Meanwhile PUFF, or sometimes called SPOOKY, arrived on the site. This was a fixed wing cargo plane retrofitted with Gatling cannons each capable of each firing thousands of rounds per minute. Multiple cannons firing created a loud groan as solid streams of red tracers resulted in some serious damage. Every fifth round on the belt was a tracer round.

The rockets were already gone. I looked toward Da Nang and watched fire balls boiling into the night sky. Incoming fire had stopped and eventually so did the outgoing fire.

During Fleet Marine Force training we were transported to the rifle range. We would shoot at targets with bullseyes. Most of the firefights in Viet Nam were when the target could not be seen. Fill the air with as much lead as possible and someone is bound to get in the way of a bullet. War is fickle. One minute it can be sheer terror and the next moment quiet calm.

"Doc, do we need a medevac?"

"No."

Battalion sent a platoon of Marines out at dawn to search the river and launch site. The entire area was bustling with pissed off Marines. In the early light of dawn, I had done a visual assessment and found a bullet had entered Danny's head just under his helmet probably when he sat up as the attack began. A Huey Chopper landed on the edge of the outpost to take him home.

Of course, the General wasn't pleased about the attack from right under our nose. The only Da Nang casualties were several jet fuel tanks. Platoon and Company sized search and destroy operations were stepped up to put pressure on the enemy. So much for an easy four months before my DEROS (Date Eligible for Return from Overseas).

The Viet Cong decided to test our perimeter the second week of February. It began with Bangalore torpedoes (long pipes filled with explosives) slipped under our perimeter wire. The torpedoes blew holes in the wire and a wave of Viet Cong charged through the holes in the wire.

Bad timing "Charlie"! The Colonel had beefed up the guard on the wire as bases throughout the country were being attacked with human waves. Half of the 105mm artillery were level and loaded with short fuse bee hives. These rounds contained thousands of tiny stainless steel darts. The darts would go through a human like a hot knife through butter. 106mm recoilless rifles and 50 caliber machine guns covered the perimeter. It was like shooting ducks in a barrel. Their RPGs were off target and they began piling up in the holes in the wire. The attack resulted in a few minor injuries, the worst being a machine gunner who accidently touched his gun barrel which seriously burned his hand. The gooks always make an attempt to drag off their dead and wounded. It becomes nearly impossible when they are laying in or on the wire.

Among the dead gooks was the barber from the market.

Staying in shape

CHAPTER XVIII

March was wet.

The rice paddies overflowed with water and the youngsters would ride on the backs of the water buffalo. The patrols and ambushes became even more of a challenge. We could either find some high ground to walk on or wade knee to thigh deep in rice paddies combined with water, piss, and shit. When we got within forty meters or so of the water buffalo, they would become extremely agitated and would sometimes charge. Americans were basically meat eaters while the Vietnamese ate rice and fish. We smelled different.

In defense, Frenchie shot a buffalo with his M-60 machine gun. When the word got back to the Battalion, they were not happy. Killing the villager's farm equipment was not good public relations. Uncle Sam had to replace the buffalo and reimburse the villager for his dead "tractor".

The Southeast Asian monsoons arrived with torrential

rain. The gooks were exposed to the same elements. Naturally, the booby traps were set on the high ground. Our wounded rate rose dramatically along with immersion foot. The skin on the feet would break open and become infected due to always being wet.

The patrol left the 1st Battalion Base at 0800 hours and followed the rice paddy dike to the foot hills. Heading north up the slope triggered multiple explosions. The Marine on point fell in a cloud of smoke while the Marine directly behind me was blown off his feet. Racing back to him I performed a quick assessment. His right leg sustained a compound fracture. Cutting his pant legs up each seam also revealed multiple shrapnel wounds to both legs. His scrotum was filleted open and one of his testicles was exposed. I applied a tourniquet on his right leg and wrapped a large battle dressing on his groin.

"Doc, you gotta get up here fast." Yelled the squad leader. Satisfied the bleeding was under control, I turned and ran up hill to the point Marine. We all wore flak jackets (armored vests) and most of us left them open in front due to the heat. The front of the point Marine's shirt was soaked with blood. He was conscious and his breathing was labored. Ripping the shirt open exposed a right chest wound. Any chest wound presents the possibility of a collapsed lung. Needing to seal the hole, I opened the side pocket of my medical bag and retrieved the clear plastic I had saved from packs of cigarettes. As I pressed the plastic over the wound and wrapped a large dressing reinforced with an ace around him, I heard the medevac chopper approaching. Leaving him, I raced down the slope and reassessed the first casualty. He was still conscious and I gave him a shot of morphine. A couple of Marines carried him up the slope just in time to load him on the chopper. The point Marine was being attended to in the chopper as it ascended and turned toward Da Nang. The booby traps had been set along the trail so when the first explosive device was triggered, the remaining devices would wipe out the entire squad. The "daisy chain" malfunctioned. I had ringing in my ears for weeks.

Returning to the base and resupplying my medical bag, I took a quick shower, and headed for the mess tent. I had the rest of the day to relax, lift some weights, and catch up on my letter writing. The following morning the Battalion Aid Station was open for business as usual. The Corpsmen assigned to the Battalion did not join the engineers for mine sweeping the roads.

Of course, we were patriotic and we had a job to do. That did not mean we were not reimbursed on a monthly basis. I had received a "battle field" promotion to the lofty rank of E-4 (Hospital Corpsman 3rd class). We were paid our grade base pay along with combat pay ($115 per month) and hazardous duty pay ($75 per month). What a deal! $190 a month for the privilege of side-stepping booby traps and ducking bullets. Some of us cashed the check for MPC (military payment certificates) and some of us sent our check home. I sent most of my checks home as there wasn't a C-Store in the 1st Battalion, 7th Marine Regiment area of operation. The stash resulted in a factory ordered 1968 Pontiac Firebird 400; a car with some serious attitude for $3200!

The assignments for the day had been posted and I was penciled in for the night ambush. No rest for the weary. The squad snaked its way under cover of darkness through the wire and walked on a rice paddy dike until we made it to the ambush site which was covered with water. Decision time. The Command and Control Center knew where we were supposed to set up as did the artillery and mortar batteries. We could spend the night sitting in the water or find a high and "dry" place where we may be exposed to friendly fire. The squad leader decided to take a chance and we set up on a knob overlooking the river. I had covered myself with a rain resistant poncho and sat down in the mud. The rain massaged my back as I faced away from the wind. Within two hours, I was soaked and shaking uncontrollably. Eventually I dozed until a Marine grabbed my arm.

"Doc," he whispered. "Clint is having some trouble."

"What?"

"I don't know."

I slowly crawled to Clint who was awake and shaking harder than me.

"Clint, what's wrong?"

"Doc, I'm having a hard time breathing. I think something bit me on the neck."

Pulling the hood of his poncho down, I felt both sides of his neck with my hands. The right side of his neck was swollen like a massive case of mumps. The swelling was cutting off his airway. Centipedes also lived on the high ground.

We had to break silence. I wasn't about to perform a tracheotomy in the rain-driven darkness.

"Call the chopper," I told the radioman.

Everyone was on full alert as I dug into the side pocket of my medical bag. I opened a small case and pulled out a syrette (a small soft metal tube with a covered needle on the end). Damn, I can't see what it is. I fumbled for my strobe and hit the on button. Morphine. That's not it. Atropine, damn. I could hear Clint wheezing. Finally epinephrine. I removed the cover and plunged the needle into his thigh. I squeezed what I hoped would be life-saving epinephrine into his muscle. I found another epinephrine just in case. I could hear the chopper approaching from Da Nang. Clint's wheezing was louder and higher pitched. The radioman touched my arm.

"They're coming in dark. Get your strobe ready."

My heart was racing. I sure didn't need epinephrine.

"Now."

I pressed the on button and the strobe sent out flashes of brilliant light.

"Off. The pilot acknowledged."

The downdraft from the blades mixed with the wind and the rain.

"He's too close! Hit your strobe!"

The shinning exterior of the chopper was feet away. We picked Clint up and slid him through the side opening.

"Go, Go, Go!"

The Medevac banked right and disappeared.

BAC S1

Chinook Helicopter

CHAPTER XIX

The brass at 1st Marine Division headquarters evidently didn't know whether to shit or go blind. They loaded a Company from 1st Battalion onto trucks and transported us to an airstrip that was lined with Chinook helicopters. Once airborne, they headed west and down the valley into the mouth of the tiger. We were given the task of blocking a large NVA (North Vietnamese Army) force from advancing on Da Nang. Okay, I guess the General is still pissed about the rocket attack. The Chinooks circled like a flock of

Mallards waiting to land in the decoys. One after one, they swooped in and unloaded Marines.

As the Chinook hovered with its rear door open, I stood in line ready to disembark. Finally, the Marine in front of me jumped and disappeared into the green vegetation. What the fuck! Too late to say, "Wait just a minute." I jumped. The elephant grass was at least eight feet high and was swaying violently from the downdraft. I landed next to the preceding Marine. He pulled me toward him and moved forward so the Marine following me wouldn't land on me. The Battalion fanned out looking for any sign. The only thing of interest the entire afternoon was a python snake. There were nearly 24 species of snakes in Viet Nam. The python was the only non-poisonous snake. I don't recall treating a Marine for a snake bite.

The next day Division changed their mind. We walked back past the previous drop zone and arrived at the airstrip where we boarded trucks, the same trucks. Maybe it was just a practice run for something much bigger. All the same, I was glad to have not met the tiger.

March was more of the same jousting. We would pretend to get involved but then we wouldn't. It was enough to give a person an anxiety attack.

April 5, 1968

Dripping dicks, most of them the same dicks, were lined up for their 2.4 million units of penicillin. I had noticed months before that officers never got the clap and they never stood in line. They would make an appointment for their "short arm" inspection and a healthy dose of antibiotic for their "bladder infection." With VENEREAL DISEASE on their record, it would be difficult rising to the biggest prick of all.

Loud shouting up the road from the BAS caught everyone's attention at sick call. As I unloaded the last syringe of penicillin into the upper right quadrant of a gluteus maximus, the shouting started to sound like a small riot. Marines were running up the road. The Corpsmen decided to investigate.

A few "chucks" were squaring off with a few "splibs". (chucks were white Marines and splibs were black Marines) Don't ask me why because I don't know. Anyway, it didn't look too serious, just a lot of shoving, pushing, swearing and talking about the other person's mother.

A senior black Marine stepped into the fracas.

"HEY, hey, what's the problem here?"

"Someone shot and killed our brother Martin."

"So, why are you fighting?"

'Our brother Martin is dead and they was calling us niggers."

"Settle down. Maybe they wouldn't call you a nigger if you weren't acting like a nigger."

Bewildered, everyone just stood and looked at each other.

"We are all brothers. We stand together, and we fall together. Never forget that. Now knock it off and act like a Marine."

The tension melted away and everyone went about their business.

The only media we would get other than letters from home was Armed Forces Radio and a military newspaper called Stars & Stripes. The assassination of Dr. Martin Lutheran King was big news for a week.

Meanwhile I listened to Adrian Cronauer on Armed Forces Radio. He was played by Robin Williams in the movie, "Good Morning Viet Nam." My favorite songs were, "We gotta get out of this place" by the Animals and "The letter" by The Boxtops.

A platoon of marines were airlifted to a French fortress on the peak of Mt. Bah Nah. The mountain was a strategic outpost. During the monsoons, the outpost was covered by low lying clouds. On sunny days the entire valley all the way to the opposite mesa (Charlie ridge) was under surveillance. Our water supply was a pool of spring water a hundred yards or so down the path from the fortress. Filling our water cans one morning, we were assaulted by incoming objects which prompted us to take cover. We soon found out it was a clan of monkeys who used the pool for a drinking hole. They were trying to drive us away by throwing rocks. In order to coexist, we changed our schedule and the problem was solved. When it came down to basics, we were able to get along with the primates but Dr. Kissinger couldn't agree with the North Vietnamese on the shape of the table during the Paris Peace Accords.

Charlie Ridge

CHAPTER XX

1st Battalion, 7th Marine Regiment, 1st Marine Division collaborated with an Army Armored Division to kick off Operation Worth. It was designed to destroy and push the enemy deep into the mountains west of Da Nang. The middle of April, the Armored Division arrived while we were making preparations. I think the Army Armored Division had more armor than the entire Marine Corps.

An armored vehicle drove up to the bank of the river. A metal bridge was folded like an accordion on top of the vehicle. The bridge slowly unfolded and spanned the river. When it settled on the opposite bank, the vehicle unhooked the bridge and drove across it. When the last vehicle had crossed the river, the bridge tender would hook and fold the span on its top and follow the column.

With the Army guarding our perimeter, we all got a good night's sleep. Reinforcements arrived the next morning to occupy the base while we were in the mountains. The Army armor escorted us to the bottom of Charlie Ridge where we set up for the night. As I was cooking my fillet of C-rations, I noticed a tracked vehicle approaching. It positioned itself among the Army armor and opened it sides to a hot Thanksgiving style meal. The Marines peered over the lids of their cans while the Army loaded their trays with hot turkey, dressing, corn, mashed potatoes and gravy.

The next morning a column of Marines slowly picked its way from the low land through the jungle up toward Charlie Ridge. The end of the column was 30 to 45 minutes behind the point. We found signs of VC activity; a small shelter, a warm campfire, and tunnels. Reaching the apex, the column turned to the west and followed the ridgeline upward to the crest of Hill 720. Now the column was in a serious traffic jam. The point was setting up a night encampment position while the rest of the Marines filtered in. I reserved a nest on the edge of the crest. Prime spot with a view of the valley far below. Once the Battalion had established a perimeter, artillery rounds were directed by fire direction control. Spotters would relay impact in meters from the perimeter and "walk" the distance 50 meters at a time toward the encampment. When the artillery was within a safe distance, the procedure would start again so the perimeter was covered 360 degrees. We could hear the report when the round was fired and soon the screaming of the projectile as it approached the target. The scream would disappear once the projectile had passed overhead. The last round at dusk sounded different. It stopped screaming well before it reached us. Everyone froze.

"INCOMING!"

I dove behind a large boulder a mille-second before the deafening explosion. Pandemonium ensued. The projectile had ripped into the triple jungle canopy, exploded and sprayed shrapnel down on the Battalion.

"God damn it. Corpsmen up!"

Picking my way through the boulders and thick smoke, a pocket of Marines was down within a 100 foot radius. The medical team sorted through the mess and began triage. Meanwhile the sun had set behind the mountains in the west and darkness moved in like a shroud. We worked feverishly with the surviving Marines. The south edge of the ridge provided just enough room for a medevac to move in close for the transport.

The Huey slipped between peaks sans running lights guided by the strobe and the radioman. The Colonel began chewing the radioman's ass.

"Are you fucking stupid? We got fourteen wounded and eight dead. Do you actually think we can get them all on that little fucking mosquito? Get a Chinook out here right the fuck now."

The medevac disappeared into the night with four of the most seriously wounded Marines. The Corpsmen re-evaluated the remaining wounded and moved them to a staging area next to the pickup site. This pickup wouldn't be easy. A Chinook loads from the back instead of the side. I sat on the north edge of the ridge while a second Corpsman was positioned on the south edge. The radioman gave me the "go" and I activated my strobe.

"Got it."

I heard and felt the downdraft of the Chinook fly over me while the Corpsman on the south edge activated his strobe. The Chinook hovered just outside the edge and slowly backed in toward the ridge. The wounded and dead were shuttled into the belly of the Chinook. One wrong step in the dark would result in slipping between the edge and the back of the chopper into the abyss.

The pilots and grunts belonged to the mutual admiration society. When they were relaxing at the air wing, the grunts were slugging it out with the enemy. When we needed them, they would never hesitate. They flew into some of the nastiest situations called a "hot LZ." But they flew out most of the time while we stayed. We were both a bunch of "crazy" bastards.

The sun also rises.

1st Battalion went quietly about its business. The Corpsmen made "house calls" on all the Marines. The plan was to send a recon team of four from our camp (hill 720) down to hill 512.

A Huey flew by. Reinforcements? Three Marines jumped from the skid and shook hands with the Colonel. They assumed a position in the middle of the ridge with an American and Marine Corps flag. While Marines were cleaning up the debris from the friendly fire, they were conducting a change of Command ceremony. Well, isn't that just perfect? There is a time and place for everything you dip shits and this wasn't it. Our old Colonel was whisked away amid pomp and circumstance and the new Colonel was now in charge.

The recon now consisted of the entire Battalion. We walked single file down to hill 512 and started the ascent to hill 841. The point man and dog handler began to see communication wire along the trail. Reporting the information back to the new Colonel, they were instructed to proceed. Another fifty yards and snipers took out both the point man and handler. The attempt for the Corpsman to render aid was unsuccessful. The German Shepherd would not let the Corpsman near his handler and the snipers had not been neutralized. Spraying the vegetation up the trail eliminated the snipers and the German Shepherd had to be eliminated. Both Marines were already dead. The Battalion attempted to return to hill 720. No luck. Now the gooks were also behind us and the tiger was ready to pounce. Thanks to Colonel Dip Shit we had no choice but to dig in for the night.

The NVA probed us the entire night and at dawn began harassing us with sniper rounds. The Colonel sent recon teams out during the day. Several of them encountered a hornet's nest and needed to be rescued. The four man recon team from hill 720 returned with three members. A Rocket Propelled Grenade round had hit the fourth Marine which detonated his entire arsenal killing him instantly. The place was swarming with gooks and they had to abandon him.

We hunkered down and spent the day watching flight after flight of phantoms, crusaders, and A-4s pound the hills around us. The U. S. S. New Jersey battleship was stationed in the Gulf of Tonkin and there was some talk about having her join the party. That idea was quickly discarded due to the artillery "snafu" (Situation Normal All Fucked Up). The strikes kept the gooks' head down while a Chinook arrived with supplies. The landing zone was really a hovering zone. The supplies were in a large net hanging from the belly of the chopper. When the net touched the open bomb crater, it was released. It contained food, water, ammunition, and mail.

I received an official looking long envelope from the Department of the Navy. Ripping it open I found my orders for my next duty station. It said, NAS Minneapolis/St. Paul. I had less than a month in country. Showing it to another Corpsman, I asked, "What the hell is NAS?"

"Naval Air Station you lucky son-of-a bitch!"

Late afternoon, I opened and ate what I hoped would not be my last supper. Top shelf C-rats included beans with weenies, pound cake, peaches and an after dinner cigarette. Each box of C-rations included a pack of four either Marlboro, Winston, Salem, or Pall Malls. Before nightfall, I grabbed my entrenching tool and dug my hole a little deeper.

Our perimeter was again probed by the NVA the entire night. Several trip flares were activated followed by Claymore mines detonating. Claymores had a couple of pins that were pushed into the ground holding the mine in place. They contained a long cord with a hand-held detonator and were designed so the blast would go one direction. Setting them up was rather simple. The Marine just needed to make sure the blast was facing outward. The Marines started putting bright orange florescent tape on the side facing them. It kept the gooks from trying to turn it around during the night.

The air strikes continued the next morning. At midday, elements of the Battalion began an assault of Hill 841. I was part of the rear element. The mountain side erupted in a continuous roar of gunfire which stalled the lead element. The afternoon was spent transporting wounded and dead Marines down to Hill 512. Air strikes were again on location. A Chinook medevac flew into the hovering zone. This time the Air Wing had gotten it right. We began loading wounded Marines into the chopper bucket brigade style. Fully loaded, the chopper flew out high over the valley and headed east for Da Nang. Minutes later another Chinook hovered in to pick up the remaining wounded and dead. As we were loading, a crew member kept screaming above the noise of the chopper.

"Move it. Move it. We gotta get out of here. GO, GO!"

I felt the chopper beginning to slowly pull up. Two Corpsmen were with me inside the chopper. For a brief second I thought about riding the bird back to Da Nang. I couldn't do it. Looking forward at Corpsman Dickenson and then at the ground, I jumped out and fell into the bomb crater. Dickenson nearly landed on me.

I looked around. "Where's the other Corpsman?"

"He's still in the chopper," he yelled.

We watched the Chinook heading for the air space over the valley when it suddenly shuddered, exploded and fell in a ball of fire.

We were all stunned. The silence was deafening. Dickenson and I finally crawled out of the crater and joined what was left of our squads.

It's payback time.

Constant air strikes the next morning finally allowed the forward elements to reach the summit. We picked our way through the smoke into what used to be a triple canopy jungle. The top of the hill was bald. The earth felt like walking on a sponge. The gooks were gone! Standing on the crest of Hill 841, the Colonel ordered squads of Marines to search the entire area for bodies. As always, the media would need numbers to sooth the conscience of politicians and protesters alike. The gooks had spent the night licking their wounds and had withdrawn taking their wounded and dead with them. The squads returned with a total of seven. The Colonel blew his top.

"Go further out. I want some dead fucking gooks."

The squad I was part of stopped just inside the jungle. The squad leader addressed the Marines.

"I don't know about you but I've had enough of this bullshit. I'm not willing to get us killed looking for ghosts. I say we go back with a 29 count."

Everyone nodded and we sat for nearly an hour before reporting to the Colonel. Evidently, the other squad leaders had the same idea. Total body count for the propaganda machine----154.

Now that's more like it!

French Outpost

Corporal Corillo's ATV's

CHAPTER XXI

So, now we had the hill. What were we going to do with it? We had paid a tremendous price for this piece of real-estate.

Well, it really wasn't much to look at anymore so we left. We followed the twisting trail through the jungle down into the valley, and turned to the East. A couple hours later, we came upon the burned out wreckage of the Chinook. A recovery mission had removed the remains at first light. The Battalion wasn't going to make the base camp before dusk so we set up shop for the night with the Army Armored unit at the mouth of the valley.

I didn't bother with a C-ration breakfast in the morning. We would be at base camp before noon. On routine patrols or ambushes, I carried a small medical bag. On major operations, the Corpsmen carried Beach Bags. They covered the entire back and weighed 75 to 80 pounds. I couldn't wait to get that elephant off my back. We cleared the tree line and the back gate of the base was in the distance. We were all exhausted and maybe let down our guard. Besides, we were just steps away and I could almost smell breakfast. The point man entered the wire at the back gate as Marines on guard duty greeted him. He was engulfed in a cloud of deadly shrapnel and smoke. The BAS Corpsmen rushed down through the wire. I took the Beach Bag off my back, sat on it, and felt like crying. He went from a proud fighting Marine to a statistic in a heartbeat.

The gooks had watched us set up with the Army the night before and knew we would be approaching the back gate sometime the next day. They planted the mine during the night. I reflected on Sergeant Green's "don't" words. Don't be predictable, don't always take the easiest way, and don't make the same mistake twice. It only made sense to use the back gate.

Didn't it?

The night after our return, the recon team who had lost a member volunteered to go back and retrieve his body. Marines don't leave their brothers behind. They left the base well after dark on what seemed like a suicide mission. They had to walk at least a mile across rice paddies, a mile into the foot hills, climb up Charlie ridge, and then to hill 720. They would search the hill in the dark for any remains.

At dawn they had yet to return. The Colonel ordered a patrol out to the foothills. Everyone was on pins and needles. The patrol returned shortly after 1200 hours with the recon team and what remains they had found. I never thought of becoming a POW (prisoner of war) or MIA (missing in action). The Marines were my guardian angels.

Three weeks left in Vietnam and I wrote my parents to tell them the good news on my next assignment. My mother had won a free phone call to me from the local radio station. I guess the station crew (who probably had a draft deferment) thought there would be a phone booth somewhere out in the jungle. She tried to use it when I was on Operation Worth(less). I think my father knew better.

The BAS continued their same daily routine. I received my flight date (May 12th). I had caught the short-timers phobia. Stories about Marines being killed just days before their DEROS were abundant. I changed my routine (don't be predictable). I kept my head down. I did my job and didn't volunteer for anything. I started getting rid of well used dirty clothes instead of washing them. I slept in my clothes. I didn't want to get caught with my pants down. I set aside a clean uniform for my departure.

On May 8 1968, an ambush from Charlie Company left the base under cover of darkness. The ambush got ambushed. A large Viet Cong force had set up a front and side shaped ambush and the squad walked right into it. After the fourth reactionary force, the siege was broken. Among those killed in action were five Hospital Corpsmen. At our morning muster in front of the BAS, the Chief Corpsman recited each name followed by a moment of silence. When roll call was finished the Chief Corpsman pulled me and another Corpsman aside.

"Get your gear and report to Charlie Company. It will be for only a few days."

"Sorry chief, I'm not going anywhere. I have my flight date which is three days away."

"Go get your gear and report to me in ten minutes. That's an order."

We walked into the Battalion Surgeon's tent.

"What can I do for you guys?"

"Sir, the chief has given us orders to report to Charlie Company as replacements for the Corpsmen killed last night. We're supposed to report to him in ten minutes.

"How long--?"

"Excuse me sir, I have three days left and Bob here has a week before we board the freedom bird for home."

"Stay here. I'll be right back."

Bob and I looked at each other and shrugged. Dr. Hines walked back into the tent with the Chief on his heels. The Chief glared at us with disgust.

"I told you to report to me in ten minutes. I'll have you court martialed for disobeying a direct order."

Dr. Hines interrupted.

"These two are not going anywhere Chief. Get the jeep and we'll go to 1st Marine Division Headquarters in Da Nang and pick up some Corpsmen."

"Sir, I gave them a direct order and I run the BAS."

"You might run the BAS Chief, but I run you. Bring the jeep around. NOW."

Dr. Hines looked at us.

"Dismissed."

"YES SIR!"

At muster the next morning, the Chief assigned us to perpetual shit detail. Corporal Corillo was still the Battalion sanitation engineer so we followed him around.

"I'm going to show you how to burn and dump shit for the next few days. So pay close tention cause Corpsmen don't seem to catch on real quick."

It really didn't matter much.

I had become so paranoid I could have been admitted to a psychiatric ward. I had decided I didn't want to ride in a jeep to the Da Nang air base. What if the engineers forgot to sweep the road for mines, or maybe they missed one. There could be snipers just waiting for me. I talked to the supply sergeant who informed me that the supply chopper was coming in on the morning of the 12th.

"Where do they go when they leave here?"

"They return to Da Nang and fill another supply order."

"Do you suppose I could hitch a ride with them to the Da Nang Airport?"

"They don't go to the airport. They go to the port of entry where the ships unload supplies. But don't worry about it, I'll have the pilot stop at the fuel depot which is at the airport."

Reporting for muster on my DEROS, Dr. Hines showed up, shook my hand and wished me good luck. The Chief didn't shake my hand. He hated me and I didn't give a rat's ass. I threw my sea bag on the mule (military ATV) and rode over to the supply tent. I had arrived way early and was becoming impatient. My paranoia had begun to slip away. What could possibly go wrong now?

The chopper ride to Da Nang was uneventful. A jeep was waiting to take me to the hanger where incoming and outgoing troops were processed. Talk about VIP treatment!

"Hey mister, you like fuckie fuckie? I get you numba one boom boom."

I had no intention of taking a souvenir home from Vietnam. I had seen enough dripping dicks in the last twelve months and mine wasn't going to be one of them.

CHAPTER XXII

The flight from Da Nang was delayed briefly due to enemy mortars from Monkey Mountain. When the plane was over the Gulf of Tonkin everyone began celebrating.

"Welcome aboard Continental Airlines. Our next stop will be Okinawa Japan."

Okinawa, Japan was a staging area before proceeding to Vietnam and back to the United States of America. Military personnel checked my orders to make sure I wasn't going AWOL (absent without leave). I joined the troops in a large building for baggage inspection. Everyone was ordered to dump their possessions on a table. The gear I had been issued for my vacation in Vietnam was now confiscated. Baggage inspection was also used to ensure black market and contraband wasn't being smuggled into the United States. Frag Phillips had been detained and thrown into the brig for trying to bring grenades out of Vietnam. He felt he needed something to eliminate the demons haunting him.

Sleep was elusive. My brain was dealing with sensory overload. A reunion with my parents and siblings, my new duty station in Minneapolis, and Cecelia. I hadn't heard from her since Christmas. Getting married immediately before deployment was never advised. Since California bases were used for deployment to Vietnam, many women would entice G. I.s into marriage. If they returned dead, the wife would collect their $10,000 life insurance. If they returned alive, they divorced them and the process would begin anew.

I must have slept because I woke up. Shaving and taking a long hot shower all of a sudden felt like a luxury. I had packed my sea bag the night before and I'm good to go. We were transported to the Kadena Air Base where we unloaded our luggage and had a hot breakfast. I left my camera in its case.

"On behalf of the pilot and crew, welcome aboard. Our next stop will be Hawaii. If there is anything we can do to make your flight more enjoyable, please let us know."

"Hey honey, I could use a little boom boom," yelled a Marine.

Loud laughter erupted throughout the plane. Beautiful "round eyed" flight attendants and troops with an overabundance of testosterone made for an interesting flight. The plane predictably touched down in Hawaii for refueling. Nobody was allowed to leave the plane.

The sun was low in the western sky when the plane landed at El Toro Marine Base in California. Another round of checking orders and luggage lasted into the early evening.

"When you leave the base you may want to get into some civilian clothes as soon as possible. Wearing your uniform is not popular with the protesters. What? No welcome home tickertape parade? No waving the Red, White, and Blue? Not proud to be a Vietnam Veteran?

YOU'RE WELCOME AMERICA!

Within two days I had been transported from the horrors of Vietnam to the streets of the United States of America. This was the birth of Post Traumatic Stress Disorder (PTSD). The challenge was to act normal, whatever normal was. Just act like nothing at all had happened. Put it all behind you and get on with living. It's not that easy. I had matured at least five years during my tour of duty. Subconsciously, I now have a choice to make. I can drown in my self-inflicted pity or I can honor those who did not survive by making something of my life. I chose the latter.

I slept like a breast fed baby. I had become accustomed to the noise of war. The roar of the jets leaving and returning to the Marine Air Wing was like a sedative. I sat up on the edge of the bed; an actual bed with a mattress and pillows. After breakfast, I called Ted and Millie. Millie answered.

"Oh honey, it's so good to hear your voice. Where are you? I'll come and pick you up right away. Are you okay?"

Millie picked me up at the base visitor's center and we drove to their home in Granada Hills, a suburb in the San Fernando Valley. Ted rushed out of the house and gave me a long tight hug. Once in the house, I was treated like the prodigal son. More hugs, food, and drinks. Eventually the conversation turned serious.

"I wish you would have written to us. I wanted to write to you."

"Cecelia has my address. You should have asked her."

"I did. She wouldn't give it to me."

Millie reached out and clutched my hand.

"Honey, Cecelia is living with our son Steve. I'm so sorry."

As I was struggling to digest the news, Ted put his hand on my shoulder.

"There is a birthday party this afternoon for her son Jimmy. He is two years old. You should come with us just to say hello. We don't need to stay long."

Ted was being generous with the cocktails. He finally

convinced me to attend the party. It probably was the whiskey. It could have been the gin.

Ted pulled into a parking spot at a single story condo complex. I was filled with turmoil. Millie knocked and walked in amid "hello grandma" and "good to see you." When Ted and I walked in, it became extremely quiet. Steve was in the sitting room reading a book to Jimmy. Cecelia was standing in the kitchen eight months pregnant.

I struggled to catch my breath. She was right when she said, "things are not going to work out between us." We just stood staring at each other. Nobody said a thing. They didn't need to as it was painfully obvious. I turned, walked out the door and headed down the sidewalk.

I threw a lot more bricks on the emotional wall I had built around myself in Vietnam. Don't let anyone ever get too close. It is less painful when a person stays busy being alone.

Ted caught up to me.

"What do you want to do?"

"I want to go home. Take me to the airport."

"Michael is coming to the party. Why don't you wait for him? He really wants to see you."

"I don't think I can. I need to go home to my family."

Ted and Millie drove to their house so I could retrieve my luggage. On the way to the Los Angeles International Airport, Millie tried to console me.

"You didn't know?"

I shook my head. "I knew something wasn't right. All of a sudden she stopped writing."

"She doesn't deserve you. I'm sorry."

EPILOGUE

Ted and Millie gave me hugs at the LAX terminal.

My family was waiting for me on the small Minnesota farm.

Maybe I'll milk a few cows, feed some chickens, and pitch a little shit.

AFTERWARD

Arriving at Minneapolis/St. Paul International Airport on May 16, 1968 I met my parents along with my sister and brother at the terminal. My hero gave me the second hug I could remember. There was a bond that would never separate us. We both shared a few tears.

A couple weeks was spent on the small dairy farm before my next assignment at the Naval Air Station in Minneapolis. I enjoyed my mother's home cooking along with the simple pleasures of life. Ice cream, cold beer, soft toilet paper, and temperature controlled showers were but a few. However, it was not always a rose garden.

I was trying to reconnect with a society that was, for the most part, too busy and too detached from what was happening in Southeast Asia to really care. I became increasingly restless. Although my mother never scolded me, my language had become somewhat salty. Not wanting to offend her I worked on cleaning it up.

Sleeping became increasingly difficult. The only noise I would hear in the night was the symphony of the crickets and frogs. Following hours of insomnia, I would dress, quietly leave the house, and walk down the dark gravel road that ran parallel to the farm. My mind started messing with me. I began hyperventilating and feeling anxious when groves of trees along the road would seem to close around me. Panic overwhelmed me and I hid in the ditch and then slowly creep back to the farm house. My father found me sitting on the porch at 5 am where I joined him as he went to the barn to milk the cows. After finishing the morning chores and a healthy breakfast, I would fall into bed dead tired.

Walking down the sidewalk in town with my father on a May afternoon an old pickup backfired near us. Leaping from the sidewalk I crouched between parked cars. He waited patiently on the walkway. Totally humiliated, I felt I had embarrassed him. Rejoined him, he acted as if nothing had happened.

Reporting to the Naval Air Station in June of 1968 I was assigned to the Medical Dispensary. The staff at the dispensary was responsible for the health of the active duty personnel and their dependents as well as keeping the medical records current of the reserves. I was living in a barracks next to the noisy airport runways where I had no problem sleeping. Within a couple months I relocated with five other Corpsmen to a house in south Minneapolis.

Life at the Naval Air Station was rather structured. After all, it was still military decorum which for some returning veterans, was a pain in the ass, but therapy for me. I had learned to never question authority. My subconscious adjustment was, for the most part, a spontaneous reaction. The 4th of July in 1968 was a nightmare. Fireworks flying high into the sky over Lake Minnetonka resulted in an anxiety crisis beyond anything I could control. Celebrating our freedom with flashes of light, explosions, and the smell of burning Pyrex had me running for the car. It would be years before I would ever attend another celebration.

One of the symptoms of anxiety syndrome is a severe startle reflex. Anyone touching me without being aware of their presence was risky business. My wife received a package in the mail containing bubble wrap to protect the contents. Without warning she began squeezing the bubbles. What sounded like automatic rifle fire sent me diving for cover from the kitchen into the bedroom. She thought it was hilarious. I did not. She accused me of abandoning her in the kitchen.

I continued and still continue to have relationship issues due to the emotional barrier I built to protect myself from unforeseen pain. However, the barrier is not as high as it once was. My readjustment from a year in Vietnam was a slow process. I made the conscious decision modern day veterans would not face the same homecoming as the veterans of Vietnam.

WELCOME HOME

THANK YOU FOR YOUR SERVICE

Home and a Squid again

FREEDOM

There are countless memorials in the United States of America honoring veterans and rightfully so. The Vietnam Veterans Memorial in Washington DC memorializes the 58,220 brave men and women who died as a result of the conflict in Vietnam.

There are 153,303 brave warriors wounded during their service to America during the Vietnam era. These numbers do not include the thousands of veterans with life-long invisible scars. They do not include the emotional scars of fathers, mothers, and siblings who still today remember their heroes who have yet to be accounted for.

The author recognizes the extraordinary heroism of the Navy Hospital Corpsmen and Army Medics who paid the ultimate sacrifice.

Freedom is not free.

PHOTOS

Heavily Fortified Communication Bunker

Children mean the enemy is not nearby.

Young boy with L.A.W.'s and Blackmarket Merchant

Future Viet Cong

ABOUT THE AUTHOR

Dell was honorably discharged November 14, 1969. He was awarded the Combat Action Ribbon, Presidential Unit Citation with Bronze Star, National Defense Service Medal, Vietnam Service Medal with three Bronze Stars and Fleet Marine Device, Republic of Vietnam Cross of Gallantry Unit Award, Republic of Vietnam Civil Action Unit Award, and the Republic of Vietnam Campaign Award.

Dell enjoyed a career as a Certified Registered Nurse Anesthetist and is now retired. He has three children, a step-daughter and five grandchildren. He is a member of the Veterans of Foreign Wars and has been Commander of his local Post three times. He is a member of the American Legion and has been on its board of directors. He is also a member of the Disabled American Veterans and the Marine Corps League.

He and his wife live in Minnesota.